Kickstarter Launch Formula

By Salvador Briggman

Introduction

We're at the beginning of a movement as transformative as the industrial revolution. Never before in history have authors, musicians, artists, and film producers been able to connect with massive online audiences and get funding for their creative work. The outdated media gatekeepers are quickly disappearing. You can now get funding directly from your fans and distribute your content online. If you're a creative type, this is the BEST time to be alive.

But, it doesn't stop there. This major change has also given rise to six and seven-figure online businesses. As a fellow entrepreneur, I know that one of the most common excuses for *not* quitting your job and launching that startup company is because you don't have the money. Now, in a few short weeks, you can have all of the capital you need to launch and grow a thriving online store.

It's no longer a *crazy idea* to pursue your passion. In fact, more and more millennials are doing just that. I should know, I'm one of them! When I first started blogging about Kickstarter in 2012, I had no idea that crowdfunding would become a multi-billion-dollar industry. I was just a Junior in college, writing a mini-thesis on how different variables affected fundraising success on Kickstarter (for you nerds out there, it was a logistic regression).

Flash forward several years, and I'm now one of the top experts in the crowdfunding industry. I started the blog, CrowdCrux, which did over one million views in 2015. I set up a forum called KickstarterForum, which has attracted over six thousand members. I even launched a popular podcast called Crowdfunding Demystified, which has racked up more than 100 positive reviews in iTunes. Finally, I also put out training videos on YouTube. I'm proud to say that the channel is experiencing rapid growth!

That all sounds impressive, but actually, when I first stumbled on the website, Kickstarter, I didn't have a clue how it worked. It seemed super confusing and I had SO MANY questions. Since

2012, I've come to master the platform and discover the ins and outs of how crowdfunding **really** works. I've published many of my findings online and I've been being linked to by sites like CNN, The New York Times, The Huffington Post, and even The Wall Street Journal.

In this guide, I'm going to share with you the step-by-step launch strategy for absolutely crushing it on Kickstarter. In no time at all, you'll be raising money for your startup or creative project. I'll make it super easy to copy and implement these tactics and strategies. I'll also share some Jedi Mind Tricks that most marketers don't know about. Before you know it, you'll be a crowdfunding expert!

Now, I bet you're thinking... "Boy this all sounds like a lot of work. Do I really have to learn all of this? I just want to get funding for my project."

Truth be told, it is A LOT to master, which is why having the right teacher can make all of the difference. I'll make sure that you master this material as quickly as possible, so that you can stop fundraising and get back to doing what you love!

Either way, whether you decide to run your own Kickstarter campaign, or outsource certain aspects, it pays to know what you're doing. I want to help you smash your Kickstarter goal and then have you on my podcast as a crowdfunding success story.

It's time to get serious about turning that business from a dream into a reality. It's finally time to get paid for your creative work. Let's get started!

- Sal

P.S. Here's the FREE Kickstarter bonus training video that comes with the guide (crowdcrux.com/kickstarterbonus).

"The effect you have on others is the most valuable currency there is." - Jim Carrey

Table of Contents

Chapter 1: What Makes Kickstarter Work SO Well

I'm not going to bore you and go over the entire history of Kickstarter or Indiegogo. However, it is important that you understand why Kickstarter works so well, the basic components of a Kickstarter campaign, and some of the common misconceptions out there about the website.

After going through this chapter, you'll have a clear idea of what you need to do to launch a successful Kickstarter campaign. In the later chapters, I'll delve more in-depth into the actual strategy for a campaign launch, along with some fundraising hacks that not many people know about.

Lesson #1: Do You Want Quick Riches?

Do want to make money *FAST*? Do you want to *GET RICH QUICK*?

Imagine receiving thousands and thousands of dollars in funds from *strangers online*!

Wouldn't it feel like you've hit the **jackpot**?

Unfortunately, the idea of quick riches and internet fame has gotten people thinking...hey...maybe I should launch a Kickstarter campaign!

I can build such and such a widget for X dollars and sell it for Y. Better yet! I can take a product that already exists and essentially run a pre-order campaign for it.

The reality: Kickstarter is not a something for nothing community. While yes, you can raise funds on the platform, you must also ship out "perks" or "rewards." You must have a high quality prototype, and you must have a compelling vision for the future.

When you set up a Kickstarter campaign, you'll be creating:

1. A pitch video, which explains the project for which you're raising funds.

2. Campaign text, which further expands on your project.

3. A fundraising duration, during which time you can accept funds for the project.

4. A fundraising goal, or the amount of money that you need to complete the project.

5. Perks or rewards, which backers have access to when they pledge money to your campaign.

We'll be going into each of these components of a Kickstarter campaign, along with others, but for now I want you to take away one thing. After you raise money, you're going to have to ship out all of the rewards that your backers have "claimed." There is a financial and time-related cost to fulfilling these rewards. You're not just getting free money.

By focusing on delivering real value to the community and making an incredible experience for your backers, you can create a launch pad that will enable you to raise funds and achieve your future dreams, whether that be wealth, fame, or making a dent in the universe.

Before I reveal the secret as to how, let's take a look at some realistic expectations for post-Kickstarter earnings. Below, I've included a few examples of how much Kickstarter campaigns raised and actually netted (profit).

Amanda Palmer's Campaign: Amanda Palmer is famous in crowdfunding circles for raising over 1 million on Kickstarter from 24,883 backers for her music project. However, just because she raised a large amount of money via crowdfunding does not mean that this lump sum translated into massive profits. In total, she ended up raising $1,192,793 on Kickstarter. But, there were costs after that huge financial raise.

The cost of manufacturing goods

$105,000: 7,000+ high-end CD-books & thank you cards cost about $15 a package to manufacture and ship.

$30,000: 1,500+ vinyls & cards, at about $20 to manufacture & ship

$80,000: 2,000+ art books (bearing in mind the shipping on those, every time they need to be shipped from the plant, to the distributor, to the backer, plus the signing).

$15-20k: Payment for design team to actually design rewards and make it awesome.

$30k: Neil and Kyle books about $300/copy for about 100 copies.

$15k: 100 turntable packages: ordering the tables, paying the artists to paint them, shipping all that stuff around.

$10k: Band tour.

$10k: House party tour.

$20-25k: Visual artists.

$150,000 of the Kickstarter money went to the commission pile. (Staff, Laywer fees, Business Manager)

$100k: Music Videos

$75-100L Kickstarter & Amazon expenses.

Amanda is quoted as saying, "If we keep our expenses down, and keep the tour pretty practical and the video budget way down, I could probably put $100k of this in the bank personally. Which would be great, but I might just be close to zero as I head off on tour this fall."

After all of the expenses, the campaign would have an estimated 8% profit. If any of the estimated costs were larger than expected, this profit would quickly erode. In my experience, it's rare that costs actually end up being less than you estimate. At best case, you may make a small profit on Kickstarter, but this could easily be chewed up if costs are more than you expected.

Miles Zuniga's Solo Record Campaign: In the DailyDot Article, "The Hidden Cost of Kickstarter Success," Fastball guitarist Miles Zuniga explained how although he raised $27,355 from 153 backers, more than $7,000 over his original goal, he forgot to account for taxes.

In short, money raised from Kickstarter and other crowdfunding platforms is considered to be taxable income. At the time, Amazon Payments, which handled the credit card transactions for Kickstarter, dispersed the funds to the project creator and sent them a 1099-K, a tax form that reports "Merchant Card and Third Party Network Payments" to the IRS.

The article goes on to explain how jazz songstress Kat Edmonson, who raised $53,823 in April 2011 to fund her second album, Way Down Low, ended up burning through the money on studio and musician payments, leaving no funds to fulfill her backer's rewards!

While yes, you may get a lump sum from Kickstarter, don't forget that it's taxable. If you estimate the costs required to deliver the project incorrectly, you may end up having to dip into your own bank account to make good on the rewards you promised your backers!

Star Command Campaign: Star Command raised $36,967 on Kickstarter from 1,167 backers for an Android/iOS game. It's the creation of indie game developer War Balloon. In an article, published on Gamasutra, Star Command shared the realities for shipping and reward fulfillment costs after Kickstarter.

Campaign Costs

$2,000 worth of pledges failed to transfer.

$3,000 went to Kickstarter and Amazon Payments.

$10,000 production of War Balloon rewards (posters and shirts).

$6,000 towards Star Command's music

$4,000 on setting up the company (attorneys, start-up fees, etc.)

$2,000 on poster art

$1,000 on iPads

$3,000 on its PAX East presence.

After these expenses, War Balloon was left with $6,000, a third of which went to taxes.

The article reports "The studio has actually taken on more than $50,000 in debt while working on Star Command, which releases to iOS and Android devices this summer."

In total, their profit was ~10%. You're not going to go laughing off to the bank from the profits made from a Kickstarter campaign. You need to coordinate reward fulfillment, shipping, deal with manufactures, respond to comments, and actually complete the project (which is not always the same as fulfilling the rewards).

This new fact that you're unlikely to make millions of dollars in profit on Kickstarter might seem disheartening, but don't fret! You don't make money on Kickstarter, you make money WITH Kickstarter. The best way I've found to explain the power of Kickstarter to non-crowdfunders is to compare it to the "Shark Tank Effect."

If you haven't seen the hit show "Shark Tank," I highly recommend watching it. Basically, entrepreneurs are invited to come on the show and pitch their business ideas/prototype products to a group of angel investors (most notably, Mark Cuban, the billionaire owner of the Dallas Mavericks).

What's incredible is that after the show, even companies that did not get deals will benefit from what is called the "Shark Tank Effect." The added exposure leads to sales, contacts from distributors, and more. I believe that successful Kickstarter projects exhibit what could be coined the "Kickstarter Effect."

From generating publicity to gathering a following, Kickstarter is an amazing tool to launch a product, attract early-adopters, and spread awareness for you and your company. I've talked with creators who have met distributors through the website that want to help them sell their product and even creators who have connected with angel investors because the campaign demonstrated proof of concept and product-market fit.

The real reason that Kickstarter works so well at raising funds for both creative and startup projects is twofold. Firstly, when a backer is pledging money to a Kickstarter campaign, they're getting access to a whole suite of rewards or perks. These backers are early adopters with disposable income and LOVE new technology that they can use or show off to their friends. These backers want this product to exist in the world and are willing to help make that happen.

The second reason that backers support Kickstarter campaigns is that they genuinely like to be a part of a new movement or trend. Think of the last time that you felt a part of a community. How cool did that feel? It's a badge of honor to say that you were one of the Kickstarter backers who helped bring the Oculus Rift into existence, which was then sold to Facebook for $2 billion.

Finally, backers actually do enjoy helping both driven creative types and passionate entrepreneurs realize their dreams. There is a tremendous sense of satisfaction knowing that it was your pledge that made all of the difference in a person's life. You directly helped to change their life forever!

Kickstarter isn't about quick riches. It isn't about "tricking" backers in any way. It's a genuine thriving community of creators and backers who are trying to bring cool new things into the world.

Lesson #2: The Pitfall of "Build it and They Will Come"

Most first-time Kickstarter entrepreneurs think that there are a bunch of strangers online just waiting to give you money. Maybe they love products or they don't have anything better to do with their lives. Wrong!

While it's true that there are regular backers on the Kickstarter platform, that is also true of major marketplaces like Amazon and eBay. It doesn't guarantee that you're going to become a millionaire or get free money. You still need an amazing product, and in this case, a well-crafted campaign.

You may think that your project is awesome and that once you put a project online, the world will beat a path to your door. This is simply not the case! The most successful Kickstarter projects put a tremendous amount of effort in the structure of their campaign, and getting the word out through the media, Facebook, and other social channels. They also work to build up an audience of fans before they launch.

It might surprise you to learn that most creators invest anywhere from 20-30 hours per week into their Kickstarter project. This includes managing the campaign, marketing it, answering backer questions, reaching out to influencers, and interacting on social media. For many, running a Kickstarter campaign is a part-time, if not a full-time job.

Unfortunately, this point is even more true today than when Kickstarter first started. Now, with so many campaigns launching every day, you have to fight to stand out above the pack. As more and more entrepreneurs begin to use Facebook ads and other advertising channels, like Instagram, you'll have to compete for the attention of regular backers. Don't worry, I'll be spending a lot of time on how to market your campaign and stand out in the later chapters.

Ironically, this growing competition is one of the reasons that Kickstarter works so well. It ensures that the platform only highlights high-quality projects. Also, when creators do marketing for their own campaign, they attract new Kickstarter backers that become a part of the platform and go on to support other Kickstarter projects.

For example, Double Fine Adventure is a video game Kickstarter project that was launched in 2012 and raised $3,336,371, bringing in 61,692 new backers. Of those individuals, 22% of them went on to back another project, to the tune of an additional $875,000 to 1,200 projects.

As another example, the famous Coolest Cooler Kickstarter project raised $13,285,226 and brought in new 4,192 backers that then went on to fund other Kickstarter projects in the weeks after the campaign finished.

The website is a marketplace of buyers and sellers. But, just because you're a part of that marketplace doesn't guarantee that the buyers will like your product or support your endeavor. You have to put in the work to make the best campaign possible.

Lesson #3: Is Your Project Right for Kickstarter?

As much as I love Kickstarter and crowdfunding, not every business and creative project is right for the medium. You'll need to go through a few different decision points to determine whether or not your project is a good fit for Kickstarter.

First, does your project fit into a specific category on the Kickstarter website? According to the Kickstarter guidelines on the company website, every project must fit into one of their categories: Art, Comics, Crafts, Dance, Design, Fashion, Film & Video, Food, Games, Journalism, Music, Photography, Publishing, Technology, and Theater.

Second, your project must result in a product or experience that can be shared with your backers in some way. This means that you can't use Kickstarter to raise money for "fund my life" type of projects, like you can with GoFundMe or other websites. If you're raising money for a nonprofit organization, that campaign has to result in a product or experience that the backers can consume or enjoy. You can't just donate the funds to your non-profit organization. As I pointed out earlier, Kickstarter is not a something for nothing transaction. Your backers should get access to perks and rewards when they pledge money to your campaign.

Third, you can't offer any prohibited items as rewards or perks. You can check out the entire list of prohibited items here (https://www.kickstarter.com/rules/prohibited?ref=rules). The list below may change, but at the time of writing, you can't offer:

- Any item claiming to cure, treat, or prevent an illness or condition (whether via a device, app, book, nutritional supplement, or other means).

- Contests, coupons, gambling, and raffles.

- Energy food and drinks.

- Offensive material (e.g., hate speech, encouraging violence against others, etc).

- Offering a genetically modified organism as a reward.

- Offering alcohol as a reward.

- Offering financial, money-processing, or credit services; financial intermediaries or cash-equivalent instruments; travel services (e.g., vacation packages); phone services (e.g., prepaid phone services, 900 numbers); and business marketing services.

- Political fundraising.

- Pornographic material.

- Projects that share things that already exist, or repackage a previously-created product, without adding anything new or aiming to iterate on the idea in any way.

- Resale. All rewards must have been produced or designed by the project or one of its creators — no reselling things from elsewhere.

- Drugs, nicotine, tobacco, vaporizers and related paraphernalia.

- Weapons, replicas of weapons, and weapon accessories.

I think that many of these guidelines are common sense. I do tend to get a lot of questions as to whether or not you can re-sell products on Kickstarter. The answer to that is no. You can also only offer rewards that have been designed or produced by you or a teammate.

The fourth consideration is that you must have a prototype if you expect to raise money through crowdfunding. This applies to both technology and creative projects. If you're going to be raising money for a comic book, you better have at least sketches, a compelling story, and artwork that you can show your backers. You won't be successful if you're trying to raise money for an idea using Kickstarter. The further along you are with your prototype, the better. This way, backers will have more confidence that you can make good on your promises, actually finish the creation, and mass produce it.

Finally, you need to put in the work to build up a small crowd before launching a crowdfunding campaign. But wait, aren't you going to Kickstarter to connect with strangers that are interested in your project? I know that building a crowd before crowdfunding sounds counterintuitive, but you absolutely must to do it. A small crowd will give you the early boost that you need to trend well in the Kickstarter algorithm, create social proof, and attract regular backers on the platform. I'll discuss this more in-depth in the following chapters. It's extremely rare that I see a creator do well when they did 0 preparation and had 0 early backers. Usually, even in those cases, they **wish** they had done more preparation, because they'd be an even **bigger** success story.

In order to get familiar with how Kickstarter works, I recommend backing a few projects on the platform. You don't have to back up the upper tiers. You could even back them for only $1 if you really wanted. By backing a bunch of trending and new projects, you'll quickly get to see how creators communicate with their backers. Pay attention to the emotions you feel as you come across the various projects, how their pages are laid out, and what backers are saying in the comments section of each project. This will be a great learning experience that you'll draw from as you put together your own campaign.

At the end of the day, Kickstarter is a community. This is one of the huge reasons it works so well as a platform to fund your creative project, tech gadget, or cool new ecommerce product. The basic campaign format also triggers many of the core human emotions that turns visitors into buyers or supporters of your crowdfunding campaign. Rather than **pleading** for money, you're providing value in return. Rather than **hoping** that people engage with your campaign when it's convenient for them, you give them a limited 30-day fundraising period where they can get their pledge in. Many of the assets of a well-crafted Kickstarter campaign, like an engaging video and high quality product photos, are the same marketing assets that work well for other types of product launches. In the next few chapters, I'll be going into the nitty gritty of launching a great campaign, along with the best practices to get the word out and stand out above the pack.

Chapter 2: Kickstarter vs. Indiegogo

If there's one thing that I want you to get out of this chapter, it's that you can actually do this. You **can** raise money for your nonprofit with crowdfunding. You'd be surprised by the number of skeptical nonprofits that I speak with. There are SO many excuses as to why it's not possible or why it's too complicated. This is simply not true, and it's probably easier than you think.

Indiegogo and Kickstarter are two of the largest rewards-based crowdfunding platforms out there. They give eligible creators the tools to raise money for projects in a wide variety of categories. In return for a donation or pledges, backers gain access to cool rewards or experiences. Fundamentally, these two sites are different from each other in a few important ways, and knowing *why* can help you choose which site will be best for your project.

Kickstarter

Kickstarter has seen a huge amount of growth in the recent years. At the time of writing, campaigns have raised 2.6 billion using their platform. With more than 11 million backers and 3.7 million repeat backers, Kickstarter is the biggest platform in the rewards-based crowdfunding space. Over 114,000 successful projects have launched on their website.

Types of Campaigns Allowed

Kickstarter is different than its competitor Indiegogo in that you can only launch an all or nothing crowdfunding campaign on the website. This means that you must hit your fundraising goal before the end of your fundraising duration. Otherwise, you won't receive any of the funds and your backer's credit cards won't be charged.

For example, let's say you launch a campaign on Kickstarter with a fundraising goal of $100,000 and a campaign duration of 30 days. At the end of those 30 days, if you've only raised $90,000, you won't be able to keep those funds and none of the backers who pledged money will have their credit card charged. All of the money will be returned to the backers.

Kickstarter places projects into the following categories: Art, comics, crafts, dance, design, fashion, film & video, food, games, journalism, music, photography, publishing, technology, and theater. Your project must fit into one of these categories.

Platform Rules and Regulations

In the past, Kickstarter has been a bit more curated and selective than their competitor, Indiegogo. They have more requirements and restrictions that you must take heed of before you hit that launch button.

Kickstarter is open to international backers, but you can only start a project from certain countries. As this list is always growing, I'd recommend looking at the Kickstarter FAQ before you decide to use the platform. At the time of writing, Kickstarter is open to creators in the: US, UK, Canada, Australia, New Zealand, the Netherlands, Denmark, Ireland, Norway, Sweden, Germany, France, Spain, Italy, Austria, Belgium, Switzerland, Luxembourg, Hong Kong, and Singapore.

You must have an address, bank account, and government-issued ID based in the country that you're creating the project in. In other words, you must be a permanent resident of one of these countries. You can also create a project on behalf of a legal entity, like an LLC or corporation. Like Indiegogo, you must be 18 years or older to create a project, unless you have a parent or teacher who is running the campaign with you.

Aside from the nitty gritty restrictions, you must also abide by a few key regulations. First of all, your project must result in an end product that can be shared with others. Usually, creators will offer this end product as a "perk" or "reward" that backers can gain access to when they pledge money. While that end product could even be an experience or event, there should be something that "happens" or "comes into the world" as a result of raising money.

Second, you can't raise money for charity on Kickstarter. This includes raising money for established nonprofit organizations or raising money to fund expenses related to your life, like education costs or medical bills. You can raise money that goes towards a project that your nonprofit is working on, like a book, but you can't just donate the funds to the nonprofit outright.

Thankfully, if you are looking to raise money for charity or to finance personal expenditures like a trip around the world, I've put together an Amazon ebook on this topic, entitled "Crowdfunding Personal Expenses: Get Funding for Education, Travel, Volunteering, Emergencies, Bills, and more!"

Also, if you want to raise money for your nonprofit organization, I've also written an Amazon ebook on this topic! You can find it by searching Amazon for the title, "NonProfit Crowdfunding Explained: Online Fundraising Hacks to Raise More for Your NonProfit."

Along with avoiding charity fundraisers, you must also avoid offering any form of financial incentives and any prohibited items. Kickstarter has a long list of prohibited items. Some of them, as mentioned previously, include: Rewards that the creator did not make, any item claiming to cure, treat, or prevent an illness or condition, contests/coupons/gambling/raffles, energy food and drinks. offensive material, offering a genetically modified organism as a reward, offering alcohol as a reward, offering financial/money-processing/credit services, offering financial intermediaries/cash-equivalent instruments, offering travel services, phone services, business marketing services, political fundraising, drugs, nicotine, tobacco, vaporizers, weapons or replicas of weapons, and pornographic material.

Notably, you also can't offer rewards of things that already exist, or repackage a previously-created product without adding anything new or without aiming to iterate on the idea in any way.

Fees That You Should Expect

If you successfully hit or surpass your Kickstarter goal, you'll be charged a 5% fee at the end of the campaign. In addition, you will pay a payment processing fee of 3% + $0.20 per pledge. If you have any pledges under $10, they'll be assessed a 5% fee + $0.05 per pledge.

Kickstarter's Campaign Ranking Algorithm

Kickstarter's platform algorithm is one reason why regular backers discover crowdfunding campaigns on the website. The algorithm will show projects that are recommended for you, those that are popular, those that Facebook friends are following, and more. On Kickstarter, there are a variety of searching options. You can search by:

- "Projects We Love"
- Recommended For You
- Saved Projects
- Trending Projects
- Nearly Funded Campaigns
- Just Launched Campaigns
- Backed By Friends
- Category
- Tags

You can then sort your search with a few different algorithms including:

- Magic Sort
- Popularity
- Newest
- End Date
- Most Funded
- Most Backed

As you can see, there are a lot of ways for Kickstarter backers to discover new projects. There are even advanced search features that will allow backers to find projects based on location! The two items that I'd like to hone in on are "Projects We Love" and "Magic Sort."

Kickstarter has always been more of a curated crowdfunding platform than Indiegogo. In fact, they used to highlight projects that were "Staff Picks." They've replaced the staff pick category with a category named "Projects We Love."

The Kickstarter website states that, *"Projects We Love is an evolution of Staff Picks, a feature we used in the past to connect creators and backers around best-in-class projects. The difference is that Projects We Love automatically get a nice little badge, so that everyone can tell when we're extra excited about a project. Projects We Love are featured by a team that works to surface extra-bright projects. They're not paid endorsements, and like any other project, they retain complete creative independence. Most simply, a Project We Love badge is a show of respect and enthusiasm from us at Kickstarter."*

Personally, I think one of the reasons they changed this is because Kickstarter creators were simply putting the "Kickstarter staff pick" badge on their project, even if they weren't chosen by the website's staff. Haha, I actually wrote a long blog post about how to become a staff pick a while back, which some of my readers may have abused. Hopefully not!

The reason that you want to become a part of this new category is twofold. First, Kickstarter sends out a newsletter every week featuring three campaigns in the Projects We Love category. Second, whether or not you're in this category will factor in to how your project is sorted in the Magic Algorithm, which I'll go over briefly next. I'll also be talking about how to get featured in the Projects We Love category in a later chapter.

For those of you who don't know, the Magic Sort is different from the popularity sort algorithm in that it *"shows you what's bubbling up right now across categories and subcategories."* The website goes on to say that the algorithm displays a *"rotating cross section of compelling projects on Kickstarter by surfacing a mixture of Projects We Love and what's popular from each of our 15 categories."* In my experience, because the Magic Sort tends to update more frequently than other algorithms, you have a higher chance of being featured here early on than through other algorithms.

As you can see, while Kickstarter does showcase projects that are popular as measured by objective metrics, they also still have the curated aspect of the platform, where they highlight projects that they themselves like! This is one big difference between Kickstarter and Indiegogo. Yes, Indiegogo does now have the "Indiegogo Team Favorites" section, but quite simply, different groups of people prefer different types of projects.

Kickstarter's Spotlight Feature

Kickstarter's spotlight feature helps creators continue to share their product's story with backers and members of the press after they've successfully completed their campaign. It also allows creators to set up a call-to-action button and direct traffic that comes to their campaign page to a website of their choice. You can customize the color, text, and URL of the button. When potential customers click that button, they'll be taken to a webpage, online store, or other location so that they can continue to pledge money to your campaign.

Next, I'll be discussing some of the features of the Indiegogo crowdfunding platform. These are key attributes that you should be aware of before you decide to launch your crowdfunding campaign.

Indiegogo

Historically, Indiegogo has been more of an open platform than Kickstarter, accepting a wide array of different projects and campaigns. At the time of writing, $950 million has been raised on Indiegogo, across all projects and across 223 countries. Over 11 million backers have donated to over 650,000 projects. In fact, on the day I wrote this very sentence, ***"7,261 contributors raised $851,210 for 1,600 campaigns."*** On the surface, they might look similar to Kickstarter, but underneath, they are quite different.

Types of Campaigns Allowed

Indiegogo offers two funding options for your crowdfunding campaign, fixed and flexible. A fixed funding campaign is also known as an "all or nothing" crowdfunding campaign. When raising money for an all or nothing crowdfunding campaign, you will only receive the pledges that you have accumulated throughout the duration of the campaign if you meet your fundraising goal. This means you absolutely must hit your goal before the clock winds down.

For example, if you have a fundraising goal of $10,000 and have only raised $9,000 by the end of your 30-day campaign, you will not receive any funds and your backers will not have their credit cards charged.

When raising money for a flexible funding campaign, you will receive the pledges that you have accumulated throughout the duration of the campaign, even if you do not meet your fundraising goal.

For example, if you raise $4,000 in 30 days with a $5,000 goal, you would still be allowed to keep the $4,000 and your backers' credit cards would be charged.

They place projects into the following categories: Animals, Art, Comic, Community, Dance, Design, Education, Environment, Fashion, Film, Food, Gaming, Health, Music, Photography, Politics, Religion, Small Business, Sports, Technology, Theatre, Transmedia, Video/Web, and Writing.

Platform Rules and Regulations

Indiegogo is much less strict than Kickstarter in terms of what you can raise money for, but there are still some restrictions. First, you can't raise funds for projects that forward illegal activities, cause harm to people or property, or for a project that scams others. Second, you can't offer certain perks, including: financial securities or incentives, profit sharing, alcohol, drugs or drug paraphernalia, weapons or accessories, lottery or gambling perks, air transportation, human remains, and any perks forwarding hate, discrimination, personal injury, death, damage, or destruction to property

Overall, you are legally bound to fulfill any promises that you make on the platform to your backers, so don't launch a campaign lightly! Also, you can only raise funds if you are over the age of 18. If you're between the ages of 13 and 17, you can use the service with consent and supervision of your parent or legal guardian.

Fees That You Should Expect

Indiegogo charges a 5% fee on all money raised on the platform. For "all or nothing" campaigns, they will only charge you a fee if you hit or surpass your fundraising goal. In addition to this fee, you should expect to pay a payment processing fee.

PayPal charges a 3-5% fee. Funds raised through credit card are assessed a 3% fee + $0.30 per transaction. If you're located outside of the USA, you'll also experience a $25 wire fee.

The Gogofactor Algorithm

Gogogofactor refers to the algorithm that Indiegogo uses to determine "Search rankings, placement on the site, featured spots in our newsletter or blog, and inclusion in our press outreach."

The algorithm is merit-based, meaning that you, as a creator, have the ability to control whether or not you optimize your crowdfunding campaign and improve its page rank on the website. Before I get into how to optimize for this algorithm, I've further expanded on what "gogofactor" is below.

"Your Gogofactor is automatically measured by the number of times you share your campaign, update your contributors, update your campaign, or refer people using your custom URL. It also measures the overall level of contributor activity, including funding, comments, and pageviews. Campaigns with a high Gogofactor are featured on our home page, in our social media outreach, and at conferences or in the press." – WatchThisIsArt Blog Quoting Indiegogo. This team raised over $6k on Indiegogo.

"Your gogofactor is a combination of many factors that measure the overall activity of your campaign along with the completeness of your pitch and media. Your gogofactor is a rolling average, so it's important to continually keep your campaign active. Your campaign is ranked relative to all of the other campaigns on the site. By staying active, your gogofactor will continue to go up. We use gogofactor as our key measure because we find that there is a direct correlation between campaign activity and fundraising success." – Indiegogo Help Center.

Key Takeaway: Indiegogo wants you to use their software and tools to keep people coming back to their website, which in turn will help you raise more funds and grow their revenue. You can optimize your campaign to make GoGoFactor work to your advantage!

The InDemand Program

InDemand is a newer program that allows creators to continue to raise money, even after their funding duration has expired. I've had creators on my podcast who have used and enjoyed InDemand and I've really come to like the idea behind the service.

Running a successful ecommerce store is the next step for many creators after hitting their crowdfunding goal. InDemand is one step in that direction and makes it easier to accept payments, get data about your audience, and to continue to build up a following.

There are a few key reasons to consider using Indiegogo's InDemand functionality and opting into the program before or after you've raised money on their platform.

First, previous success establishes credibility among new customers. Gaining credibility in the eyes of potential customers, backers, and crowdfunding enthusiasts is one of the hardest parts of preparing a new Indiegogo campaign. After you've hit your goal and already done the work to market your project and develop a core following, it's the perfect time to capitalize on the credibility that you've worked hard to build up. Indiegogo's InDemand program is one way to do that.

Second, launching an ecommerce store comes with expenses anyway. Whether you are planning to set up an ecommerce store with Shopify, Magento, or Wordpress, you're going to have monthly expenses. This could come in the form of transaction fees, PayPal fees, credit card processing fees, software fees, website design costs, or website hosting fees. When you first think about it, the 5% fee that Indiegogo charges (plus payment processing) sounds expensive, but it really takes away a lot of headache and you're getting a good amount of functionality.

Third, you can use Indiegogo's InDemand program to continue to share your story. As you'll learn in future chapters, marketing is all about telling your story through different mediums. On Indiegogo, you have the opportunity to share who you are, what you're about, and why your product matters through your video, text, description, and title. These elements are still customizable after you finished your campaign. New customers who arrive on your page can see how your story has progressed over time, which is pretty cool!

Fourth, you can continue to build your community on Indiegogo. You see, in the past, I've been guilty as much as anyone else when it comes to obsessing over growth metrics, financial numbers, and statistics. But that's not what matters. Every new pledge is not just a number in your database. It's representative of an actual human being, with thoughts, feelings, aspirations, and friends. The comments section on your project page, updates, your video, and your campaign text are all ways to continue to build a relationship with the community that has formed around your project. Your Indiegogo page is a centralized place, similar to an online forum or Facebook group, where backers who have similar interests can interact, ask questions, and provide suggestions as to the direction of your project.

Fifth, you can use your Indiegogo page to capitalize on SEO. New websites take time to rank well in search engines. Even if you're just trying to rank for your brand or company's name, it will take time. If you mention your brand name to people that you meet at a conference or at a coffee shop, it might be difficult for them to find your website online. Your website might also not be fully fleshed out and you might not have the right content necessary to convert a passive visitor into a customer. It's likely that your Indiegogo campaign page is ranking pretty well for the core terms related to your brand. If you're accepting new backers through the InDemand program, then you'll be sure to not lose out on any sales!

Sixth, opting into InDemand will help you maintain your momentum. Some crowdfunding campaigns experience what appears to be exponential growth throughout the duration of their project. This means that over time, more and more backers keep discovering their campaign page, leading to pledge growth and runaway fundraising success. Opening your project up to new backers is one way to harness the power of this momentum. I would also look into stretch goals as a way to appeal to new backers. Remember, you might still be in the Indiegogo marketplace, but you need to market your project to take advantage of this period between your crowdfunding success and setting up your own ecommerce website.

Lastly, you can continue to collect analytics. The more you deeply understand your customers, the better your chance of developing your company into an industry leader and beating out the competition. Ideally, you should gather analytics on customer behavior from your own website and email list, but for the time being, you can use Indiegogo's platform to get a feeling for which tiers customers love most and where they're discovering your project from.

You Can Include A Secret Perk

What's an Indiegogo secret perk? Basically, it's a way to reward loyal supporters! You can provide a unique link that will unlock a "secret perk" which they can choose when they back your campaign.

Not only can you use a secret perk to thank your hardcore followers, but you can also use it when courting bloggers, influencers, and online communities to get them interested in your Indiegogo campaign.

No one wants to feel like they are being marketed to. The goal is to make your followers feel unique, special, and valued. The secret perk is one way to accomplish this.

Which Platform Should You Choose?

Ultimately, this answer comes down to the needs of your business or creative endeavor. As you can see, each platform has different functionality. On average, Kickstarter does have a larger community and the site gets more traffic than Indiegogo. However, I've had many creators who have talked about how the Indiegogo team reached out to them and that they appreciated the personal touch. I've even talked with some creators who launched a campaign on Kickstarter and then transitioned it to the Indiegogo InDemand once they had successfully raised funds.

For the rest of this guide, I'll be exclusively focusing on Kickstarter and strategies to maximize the success of your project. We'll be discussing a lot of different topics including marketing, PR, fulfillment, and of course, how to actually get backers. Thankfully, many of the tactics I'm about to go into are also applicable to Indiegogo! But, before I actually get into those topics and nail down how to drive traffic and sales to your campaign, I'm going to show you how to create a prototype. This could be a prototype for a creative work or a product. Either way, you're going to need some type of work to show your backers to convince them that yes, you can actually deliver on the rewards or perks that you promise in your campaign.

Chapter 3: How to Create a Prototype

Every great physical product starts with an idea. Every massively successful Kickstarter campaign first started out as an idea in an entrepreneur's mind. There are many steps that you must take towards launching a successful ecommerce store, but turning your idea into a prototype is the most important part. It's that initial step that sets you out from the pack and thousands of wantrapreneurs who have "revolutionary ideas," but fail to take action. Let's go through some of the things that you need to keep in mind when you're creating your first prototype!

Step #1: Sketch it Out on Paper

When I tell people to sketch their product idea out on paper, most look confused. In an era of computers, smartphones, and impressive software technology, why would you waste time with an old-school piece of paper? There is a time and place for fancy drawings, but for now just get a rough idea of the product that you'd like to make by sketching it out on a blank piece of paper. You can just use simple graph paper and a black pen.

Creating a concept sketch is the very first step towards making a full-blown prototype that you can interact with and show to investors or users. The reason it's the first step is because it's quick, it's easy to do, and it's cheap. You'd be amazed at the questions that will pop up in your mind once you take the time to commit your idea to paper. It will be easier to pinpoint which aspects of the product you're still fuzzy on, and which ones need further thought.

It's best to make several sketches to fully grasp what the product is going to look like from multiple angles. How will the product sit on a table? How will a user interact with it? Depending on the product, you might add 3D views as you're sketching, before you fully transition it over to a software program.

Step #2: Use Software to Create a Design File

While yes, you can bring basic sketches to a design firm or company that will help you get the prototype made, you'll get a more realistic version of what you want if you use a software tool first. You can show those designs to teammates, investors, and design companies. You'll be able to easily manipulate the designs and create multiple versions. There are a few different tools that you can use to really flesh out your design. I'll be covering a few of them below.

Adobe Photoshop: This is a great software program that you can use to transition your drawings from paper to the computer. Adobe Photoshop is one of the most popular options out there. It contains a lot of rich functionality that will make your job easier. You can also get the Creative Cloud, which includes Photoshop, Illustrator, InDesign, and more.

Adobe InDesign: Similar to Photoshop, you can use InDesign to bring your product sketch to life! Of course, it will take a bit of time to learn how the software works, but the skills you learn will pay off big-time in the long run.

Balsamiq: While Balsamiq is primarily used for creating wireframes for software products, it's another option that you could use to copy your sketch to the computer. It's another good option if you don't want to invest in Photoshop.

Once you get your sketch onto the computer using a software tool like one of those mentioned above, you'll then need to make a 3D rendering of the product. This file is crucial for the prototyping phase, as it will determine the various measurements for the product. There are a lot of software tools out there that will help you do this. I'll mention a few below.

Tinkercad: Tinkercad is super easy to use and way less complicated than CAD. It's a great software tool for making the 3D rendering for your product, along with all of the measurements and specifications.

CAD: CAD is more of a professional solution, especially if you already have some familiarity with designing and prototyping new products. If you're a professional designer or architect, you've likely heard of and use CAD.

SketchUp: SketchUp is another 3D modeling software that will help you bring your drawings to life. You can export your drawings as PDF, images, or CAD files.

Once you have a 2D and a 3D design file for the product, you're one step closer to bringing a whole new product into the world. I know that it sounds like a lot of work and planning, but the more thorough you are with this phase of product development, the lower the chances of design or manufacturing mistakes. In the next section, I'll be going over a few ways that you can turn that design file into an initial prototype of the product.

Step #3: Pick a Way to Get it Prototyped

There are a lot of ways to turn that 3D design file into a physical object. Before you actually go about making the prototype, you should ask yourself what your goals are with the prototype, including function, needs, and features. Do you need a fully functional prototype? Are you seeing how the user will interact with it? Having a goal will help you decide which method of prototyping to use. This decision can save you considerable time and money.

First of all, if you don't need much functionality and you're just trying to get an idea of what the product will look and feel like, you could create a quick cheap prototype using one of the products below:

Shapelock: You can use Shapelock to make parts, brackets, molds and more. The plastic material melts in hot water and then locks rigidly at room temperature. It's easy to mold with your hands can be used to make a rudimentary prototype. You can also use InstaMorph, which is an alternative to Shapelock.

Sugru: Sugru is moldable glue that you can use to fix items around the house or prototype a product. It's flexible, "grippy", adhesive, and durable. Depending on your product, you can use this glue to make an initial prototype.

Sculpey: Sculpey makes innovative clays that you can use to sculpt into a prototype of jewelry and other items. It's a similar compound to Shapelock and Sugru, making it perfect for rapid prototyping.

Foam: Finally, you could also create a foam prototype! Foam is easy to work with, cheap, and relatively durable. You can use Foamcore to create a model or a life size prototype of your product.

But, I admit, these are quick and dirty rapid prototyping options. If you're looking to get a more realistic idea of what your end product will look like, you could also use 3D printing to cheaply create a prototype for your product, using a site like one of those below.

Shapeways: Shapeways lets you upload your design file directly to their website and choose from a variety of materials. You'll get instant pricing and be able to easily get an idea of what your finished product will look like.

Sculpteo: Sculpteo is another service that will render your 3D printed creation and ship it out to you in the mail. You can quickly see what your finished product will look like.

I.Materalize: I.Materalize is a third online service that you can use to get a 3D printed creation of your product. Just upload your 3D design file, specify materials and color options, and you're set to go!

Buy a 3D printer: If you want to learn a bit more about 3D printing and think you're going to get a lot of use out of the machine, you could also consider purchasing a 3D printer!

Finally, you could also look into getting the product made through CNC milling, especially if you want to incorporate production-equivalent materials. You could also research injection molding if you want a large number of prototypes made from production-equivalent materials.

Step #4: Iterate and Repeat

Finally, once you actually do get your first prototype made, the process doesn't end there! Likely, you're going to have to re-work the product and repeat the prototyping process. Maybe you realized that it's difficult for the user to hold the prototype, or that you left out some key bit of functionality. Either way, remember that this is all a learning process. You're collecting as much data as possible in terms of how the user interacts with the product, so that you can create a better experience for your paying customers.

Once you learn how to prototype a product, the effect is extremely powerful! You'll be able to show that prototype to partners, customers, and potential investors. Your idea is no longer in your head, it's in your hands. You're one of the few inventors or designers who actually took action and got their product made.

When you get to a point where you're happy with the prototype, you've identified manufacturers, and you have a plan for fulfilling customer orders, it's then time to consider launching a crowdfunding campaign to finance your initial production run. In the next chapter, I'll be breaking down what goes into an effective Kickstarter campaign that successfully raises money from the crowd.

Chapter 4: Making a Great Campaign

I'm not going to lie. The makeup of your crowdfunding campaign has a huge impact on whether or not you're able to successfully raise money online. Even organizations who have a devout following and strong brand recognition still need to put together a well-constructed campaign page. But, there's so much more.

Kickstarter campaigns are launched every single day. But, not all of them successfully raise funds. In fact, Kickstarter campaigns only have a 35.79% success rate. That means that the majority of crowdfunding campaigns out there are not going to raise money online. I want to help you be a part of that small group of campaigns that successfully raise money from the crowd. By following the crowdfunding best practices that I've shared below, you'll be far more likely to absolutely smash your Kickstarter goal.

Lesson #1: Don't Put Your Needs First

Ironically, although we live in a highly individualistic and egocentric society, the individuals that prosper most economically are those that put other's needs, wants, and desires before their own. You think I'm joking?

Pick out a problem, need, or want that everyone faces. Let's say the desire that most people have to feel like they can reach their potential and be in control of their own life. Now, imagine an author that writes a book that inspires millions of individuals to take action and strive to live out their dreams. From having read this imaginary book, people end up having a better quality life, are grateful, and are more than willing to pay another $10 for the author's next book, or even recommend the book to a friend.

Although the author invested time and energy into producing the book, it is only after it has become helpful for another, that he or she prospered. By making it your primary motivation to add value to other people's lives, you will receive dividends well into the future.

I know that YOU want to raise money for a project that YOU believe should exist in the world. That's awesome! You're taking the right initiative to turn your dreams into a reality. However, if other people don't experience this pain point that you're trying to remedy or recognize the brilliance of the project you're trying to complete, it's going to be very hard to get Kickstarer backers.

Ask yourself, how does this product benefit *other people*? How will this product benefit other people's lives? How do I know that these assumptions are true? When you begin to find the answers to these questions, you'll be able to craft a compelling message that will turn campaign page visitors into backers!

Lesson #2: Research Popular Kickstarter Campaigns

Whether you're planning to be successful on Kickstarter or with any other endeavor, it's crucial that you research other individuals who have been successful in the same arena and what elements contributed to their success. By researching similar Kickstarter campaigns using the steps below, you can determine the best source of pledges for your category, where you should concentrate your PR efforts, and how to best allocate your marketing budget. As an example, I will analyze the Mogics Light Kickstarter campaign below.

The Mogics Light Kickstarter campaign ended up raising a little over $60,000 from 2,000+ backers to create a revolutionary multi-functional light. The campaign showed more of a linear pledge growth model over the span of 60 days (talk about maintaining momentum!). When taking a look at this campaign, the first thing that you can do is use the website Kicktraq to gain some insight into their campaign's analytics.

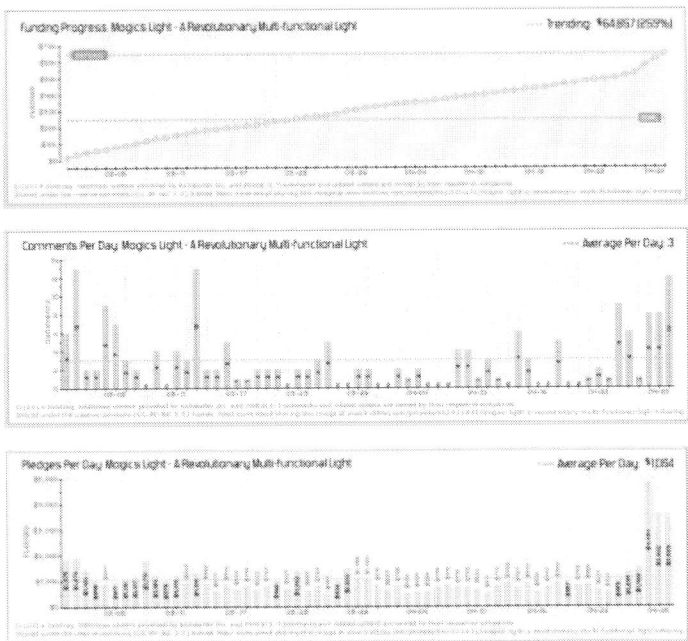

This information will give you a benchmark for your Kickstarter efforts. It seems like there was a big rush towards the end of the campaign and steady progress each day throughout the duration of the 60 days. There was an average pledge of about $1,000 per day and an average of 3 new comments added per day. You can dig deeper into these statistics by looking at the Kickstarter community tab.

The Kickstarter community tab shows:

- The cities where backers come from
- The countries where backers are from
- How many new vs. returning backers supported this project

- A breakdown of the different people supporting this project

I took a look at the data for this project and discovered that while the majority of backers came from the USA (1,138), the top cities where backers came from was Singapore (53), London (39), and New York (32). They received nearly half of their backers from international locations, including UK, Germany, Australia, Canada, and more. Finally, they attracted 1,891 backers who had ***already backed*** a Kickstarter project in the past and 137 who had never backed a campaign before.

This data tells me a lot of things, especially if I have a similar product. Most importantly, if I had never factored in international shipping costs, that's something I'd need to look into before launching my project. Should I decide to do Facebook ads, I now have a few different ways that I can create a target audience that is likely to convert into backers. Finally, since this project received pledges from backers who have supported a Kickstarter project before, I can have more confidence that my product might appeal to regular backers on the platform.

If you'd like to get a quick snapshot of where backers came from for this campaign, you can also take a look at the Bitly analytics for the Kickstarter short link. Just click the Twitter share button on the project page, get the short link, and then add a "+" to the end, which yields "http://kck.st/1dJk91x+". You'll see data similar to the images below.

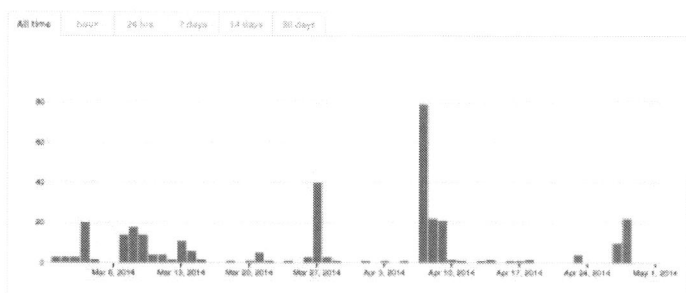

Geographic Distribution of Clicks

This information will give you an idea of where the traffic for a campaign came from and from which locations around the world. You can use it to further inform your marketing strategy going forward.

While researching a project, you should also look into the volume and type of PR attention that they received. You can simply use Google for this. By typing the title of the Kickstarter campaign into Google and filtering by content type and time, you can create a media list of all the websites that a campaign managed to get on. You will also discover if the creator did any forum promotion or posted on any social bookmarking websites. I decided to search by the "custom range" of Feb 15th, 2014 to May 1, 2014 (two days after they ended). This came up with a bunch of publications. I've included a few below

- http://www.trendhunter.com/trends/mogics-light

- http://innovation.uk.msn.com/tomorrow/best-new-inventions-for-march?page=5

- http://www.meecouk.co.uk/news-overview.php?news_id=181

- http://www.geeky-gadgets.com/mogics-multi-functional-light-video-24-03-2014/

By doing this research, you're creating the beginnings of an outreach list. You've identified a few online publications that were receptive to writing about this product. They'll be great publications to pitch leading up to the launch of your own campaign.

It's very difficult to know how you are doing without some kind of a benchmark. This applies to Kickstarter and your own business endeavors. Any goals you set must be made in the context of a dataset that is realistic. Otherwise, you could be setting unrealistic goals or you might think you are doing horribly, when you are actually above the average. Therefore, you should also research the number of video views that successful and not so successful crowdfunding campaigns receive.

Unfortunately, there isn't an easy way to get video view data for other Kickstarter projects without directly reaching out to the creator (If there is, let me know via comment!). If you are researching similar campaigns on Indiegogo, creators use YouTube or Vimeo for their project videos, and you can get a sense of the stats for these mediums using the tools below.

Gosnell Movie

A historic crowdfunding campaign for a movie about America's biggest serial killer, abortionist Kermit Gosnell and the media cover-up.

Los Angeles, California, United States   78m

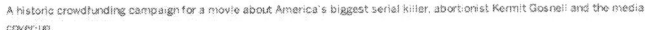

Story | Updates 29 | Comments 499 | Funders 25,338 | Gallery 17

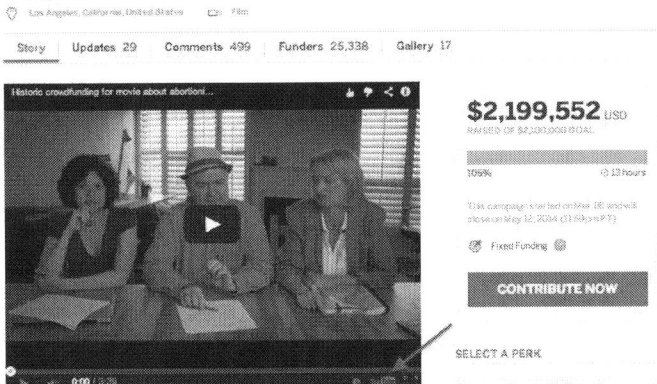

$2,199,552 USD
RAISED OF $2,100,000 GOAL

109%   13 hours

This campaign started on Mar 30 and will close on May 12, 2014 (11:59pm PT)

Fixed Funding

CONTRIBUTE NOW

SELECT A PERK

YouTube

Historic crowdfunding for movie about abortionist Kermit Gosnell

Phelim McAleer 71 videos

Subscribe 3,227   64,116

                                              292   29

Like   About   Share   Add to

37

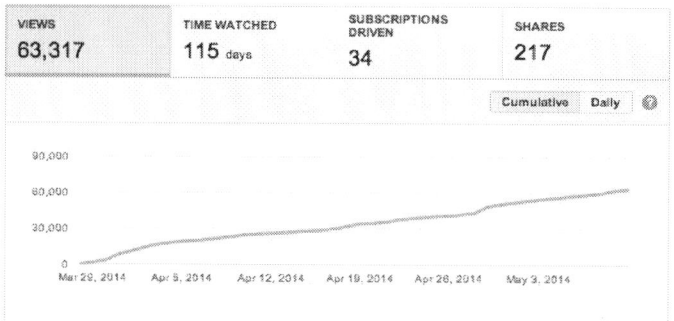

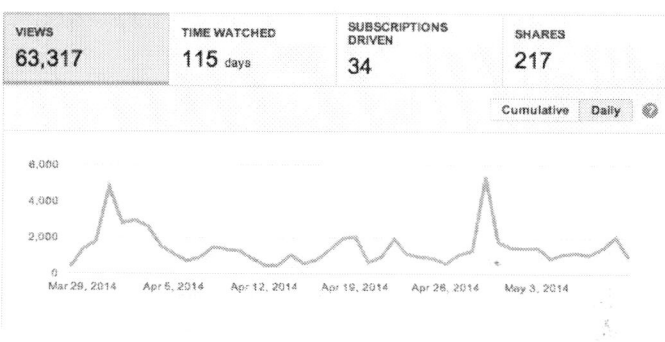

GOkey: Charger. Cable. Locator. Memory. All on your key-ring.

Boost your phone battery, use it as a charging/ syncing cable, store your data, locate your keys and find your phone.

◎ San Francisco, California, United States   ▭ Technology

Story | Updates 1 | Comments 162 | Funders 2,910

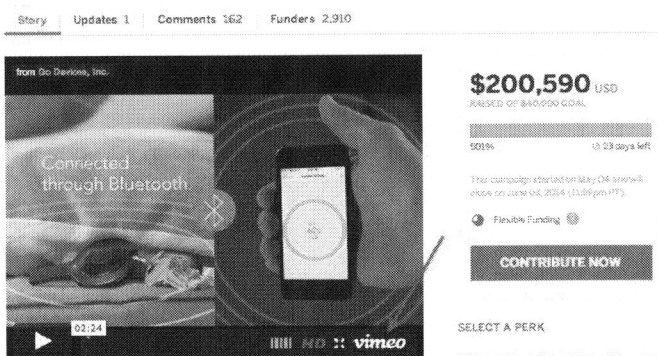

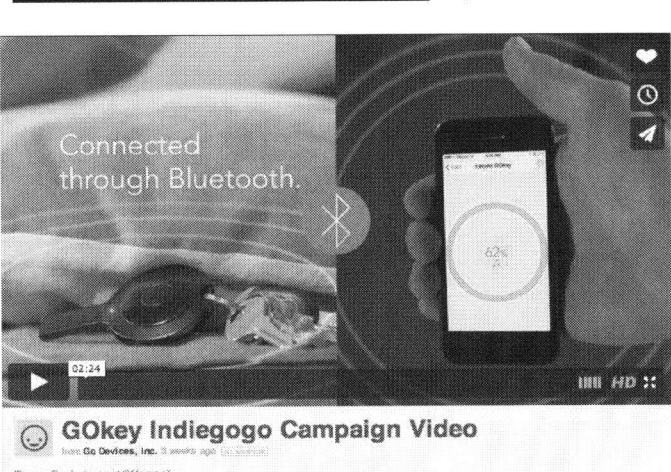

GOkey Indiegogo Campaign Video

from Go Devices, Inc. 3 weeks ago

Becca Goebel – cast "Woman"
Peter Oren – cast "Man"
Jayse O'Brien – cast Voice Over
Doros Kiriakoulis – Spokesperson/ Producer/ Director
Ben Ferrer – Cinematographer/ Editor benferrer.com
Ilena Ferrer – Line Producer/ 1st AD
Brian Herezog – Grip/ Electric

Read More...

✓ Follow   ⋯ Stats

39

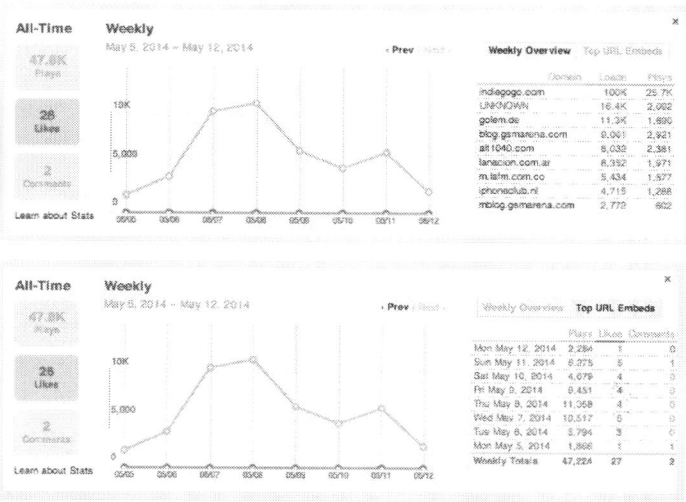

Finally, I would look into the social media chatter that has bubbled up around the project. There are a few ways to do this. One way is with the Twitter Advanced Search feature. You can experiment with putting the campaign's keywords into Twitter Advanced Search and see what kind of Twitter response they received. You'll be able to see who tweeted, how often during the campaign, and more. You could also put in the exact phrase "I just backed Mogics Light – A Revolutionary Multi-functional Light on..." to see which Twitter accounts backed the campaign. This will give you an idea of the organic social media marketing around the project.

Another way is with the software tool Buzzsumo. Using Buzzsumo, you can input keywords, phrases, or terms, and discover content that is going viral on Facebook, LinkedIn, Twitter, Pinterest and Google+. You can then use that information to create a media list of the blogs and news sites that are writing about those key phrases. When you do a search, you can filter the results by content type (infographic, article, guest post, interview, etc) and date (past 24 hours, week, month, etc). You'll be able to see how many shares each piece of content received and also filter the content by number of shares on a particular network or total overall shares.

This information is amazing if you're trying to create a media list of blogs or news sites to approach. You can see which ones have the biggest clout in niche industries and also discover ones that might not have been on your radar. Finally, you can export this entire list to CSV and it is automatically segmented by the header titles! What's even more helpful is that you can click on "View Shares" for a particular PR hit and get a list of all the people on a particular network that shared that link. I'll be talking more about Buzzsumo in the section where I talk about getting the media to write about your product.

As you go about researching Kickstarter campaigns that are similar to yours or that are in the same category, keep in mind that you can always reach out to the creators of these projects. Don't be afraid to shoot them a message and ask them a question. You'd be surprised that some are actually very helpful. In addition, I'd highly recommend backing a few projects, even at the lower reward tiers. You'll get a first-hand view of how campaign management is done. If you back both successful and not so successful projects, you'll see how the marketing differs between the campaigns, as well as the creator's communication strategy.

Lesson #3: Validate Your Project or Product Idea

This might seem counterintuitive. You might have been planning to launch a Kickstarter campaign to figure out whether or not there is demand for your project or product. If a bunch of people ended up backing your campaign, you'd allocate more time and resources to that product. In the early days of crowdfunding, we did see some campaigns that seemed to be "magically funded," but now-a-days, you must validate your product before going on Kickstarter. You must do your homework and customer research before you launch.

If you've never read the book, The Lean Startup, by Eric Ries, put it on your wish list! The Lean Startup is considered by many entrepreneurs to be as monumental to the world of startups as the ideas of testable hypotheses, independent/dependent variables, and controlled experiments were to the scientific revolution.

In this book, Eric Reis the cofounder of IMVU, a social entertainment website that has over 100 million registered users, argues that rather than relying on entrepreneurial hunches and intuition to spur the development of new products, creators should apply the scientific method and conduct trial-and-error testing to figure out the products or marketing strategies that best resonate with customers. In addition, Reis argues that validated learning is more important than initial revenue for startup companies.

That last concept seems really strange, so let me elaborate. Let's say you want to create a new website that allows students all over the world to exchange or sell used textbooks for a small fee. Why should students sell their textbooks back to the university bookstore, which pays pennies on the dollar for expensive studying materials? Why not cut out the middle man?

You begin looking up statistics regarding the number of used textbooks sold all over the world, the number of students attending colleges/universities, and you start to realize how many subjects and curriculums overlap. Wow! This textbook exchange website begins to seem like a huge market opportunity. So what do you do?

Maybe you put together a really nice pitch deck that you show to investors, and since you're a senior manager at a well-known company, you have the reputation and credibility from running other people's businesses to raise a good chunk of capital.

You go about spending your newly raised funds. You hire programmers, salespeople, customer support, and invest in company infrastructure. It might seem like you're spending a lot of money, but since the market is SO large and you only need a small portion to become cash-flow positive, you're not worried.

After 8 months, you launch your crisp software product, roll out ads on all the major platforms, get some news coverage, get a lot of traffic, and... no one uses the product.

You've spent a small fortune discovering a simple lesson. Maybe textbooks are not as much of a pain point as you imagined, up-to-date editions matter more than you expected, or there wasn't nearly enough activity to cover your monthly costs, and it might take another few million to even find out if you can get that amount of activity. Essentially, you've learned some lessons at a great cost.

This is a long way of saying that learning about your customers is the foundation of long-term growth. The quicker you are able to test your assumptions about your customers, be they readers of your new book, players of your game, or users of your software product, the better. I'd recommend grabbing a sheet of paper and writing down all of the assumptions that you have about these people who you expect to support your Kickstarter campaign. Include assumptions that you have about their lifestyle, problem, interests, and where they congregate online. You can even go so far as to ask yourself who they would consider authoritative sources of news? Where do they find out about new products that they care about?

Over the next few weeks, make it your job to test each one of these hypotheses. As you go through this list, you'll be gaining a more in-depth view of who will back your Kickstarter campaign and how you'll communicate to this audience. If you do nothing else, test the #1 core assumption that all Kickstarter campaigns have, which is that someone will actually buy your product. There are a few different ways that you can do this. I'll flesh out one way.

First, you're going to need a product landing page. This landing page will contain persuasive information about your product to "sell it" to any visitor. There will also be a "buy button" so that visitors can express interest in owning the product. You should make it so that there aren't any other links on the landing page. The only decision that a website visitor has is to buy the product or click off your website. There are a lot of different software tools that you can use to create this landing page, like Leadpages, OptimizePress, Unbounce, and Wordpress. It doesn't matter which tool you use to make it. What does matter is that you have analytics installed on this landing page.

Depending on the provider that you go with, you can use the analytics provided by the software tool or Google Analytics. For this example, I'll be talking about how you can use Google Analytics to validate a product idea. Make sure that Google Analytics is installed on your website, so that you can track where visitors are coming from, how long they're spending on your website, what type of device they're using, and more. Once you have it installed, set up a conversion goal, so that when someone arrives at a certain destination, like a checkout screen, you'll be able to track that conversion.

Now, you'll be able to track and see when a website visitor decides to buy your product. This is referred to as a conversion. You can use this information to decide whether or not to launch a crowdfunding campaign for your product. You can also put a revenue value on each of those actions, like $50. If you send 500 visitors to that landing page through paid or organic traffic, and 50% of those visitors decide they want to own the product, that's $12,500 in potential pledges. Using this technique, you'll quickly be able to see whether or not it makes sense to pursue this product. You can also play around with the wording and images on the landing page to see how they influence your conversion rates.

Once you have validated your hypotheses and your product idea, you'll know for sure that it's a good idea to invest your time and energy into launching a Kickstarter campaign! This will make you feel much more comfortable when marketing the product, or investing in advertising. Next, it's time to consider what the costs will be of actually running a crowdfunding campaign.

Lesson #4: Estimate Campaign Costs Correctly

There's nothing worse than raising money on Kickstarter, shipping out all of your rewards, and finding out that you actually lost money on the entire campaign. Maybe you forgot to calculate shipping accurately, or didn't take taxes into account. For whatever reason, you are now in debt. Don't let this happen! By calculating costs carefully before launching your crowdfunding campaign, you'll make sure that you come out ahead. First, let's talk about taxes.

The implication of taxes when running a Kickstarter or Indiegogo campaign is a huge gray area for most creators. The reason the question is so difficult to answer is that depending on your home country, state, and industry, the answers may vary enormously. In addition, how you use your Kickstarter or Indiegogo funds and what they were raised for can have a big impact on the taxes you must pay.

Please keep in mind that I am not an accountant and any of the resources I provide below should not be construed as tax advice. They are simply meant to help you navigate the crowdfunding waters. I always recommend that if you are uncertain, you should consult an accountant. I will be primarily focusing on US tax implications.

In general, the funds received on Kickstarter or Indiegogo can be classified as income or a non-taxable gift. Sometimes, certain portions of your funds raised, like money exchanged for product-tier rewards, can be classified as income, and other portions, like donations, may be classified as a non-taxable gift. I'll break down the differences and definition between these classifications.

For most campaigns on Kickstarter, the majority of pledges will fall into the income category, as the website forbids charity fundraisers. On Indiegogo, I still think the majority of pledges will fall into this category, but there are likely more that could fall into the "non-taxable gift" category, particularly if you're running a campaign on Generosity.

According to CrowdfundCapitalAdvisors, "If the rewards issued are tangible and comparable to what the market price would be for that good, then it is a business transaction, and any profit derived from the sale is considered taxable income."

This means that if you are raising money for a cool new watch and are offering the watch or accessories for the watch as perks for a price that is comparable to its retail price, then any profits made from those pledges would be considered taxable income.

If you own a registered business and are running the campaign under your business, you would file the income accordingly (LLC, Corporation, etc). If you do not own a registered business or are not running the campaign under your business, then you would likely be classified as a sole proprietor and need to pay the applicable sole proprietor federal, state, and local taxes (along with any licenses you may need to operate).

Other pledges might fall into the non-taxable gift category. There are two circumstances where pledges received could be considered gifts:

1. A backer pledges and chooses not to receive a reward.

2. A backer pledges and the reward is diminutive compared to the amount given (considered a gesture of gratitude).

"For example if a funder were to donate $50 and they were to receive a mug or a calendar as a thank you, this would not count as a transaction but rather a gift," says CrowdfundingCapitalAdvisors.

Currently federal law exempts the first $14,000 of gifts made during the course of the year to anyone other than a spouse from the federal gift tax (this amount is indexed for inflation but can only increase by $1,000 increments).

Aside from calculating potential income tax, you'll also have to look into how sales tax will affect your crowdfunding campaign. I would highly recommend researching sales tax, in particular internet sales tax, in your state. If you google "internet sales tax" the first result that comes up is a helpful 50 state guide to state sales tax laws. As you can tell from that website, it really depends on the state you are living in. Let's take New York for example. "The current default rule throughout the United States is that you must collect sales tax on Internet sales to customers in those states where your business has a 'physical presence.'

For guidance on how physical presence, or nexus, is understood specifically under New York law, consult Section 1101(b)(8) of New York's tax laws (N.Y. Tax Law). The section provides a relatively lengthy set of statements defining "vendor," which is a person or other entity required to collect and pay sales tax. Several definitions of "vendor" now involve "affiliated persons." In addition, New York's definition of "vendor" includes:

- a person who solicits business by distributing catalogs or advertising, "if such person has some additional connection with the state which satisfies the nexus requirement of the United States constitution," and the person makes sales of taxable items within New York

- a person who makes sales of taxable items and "regularly or systematically" makes deliveries of those items into New York other than by common carrier (i.e., not using U.S. Mail, UPS, Fedex, etc.)"

This interpretation is not the same for every state. You must do your research. If you have backers located in your state or elsewhere, you may need to pay sales tax! Regardless, I would highly recommend including a location field in any surveys you send out, so that you know where your backers reside.

While you'll be keeping track of these expenses yourself, you'll also get a 1099-K tax form if you're a US creator. This form should come from Payable, a tax-filing service that has partnered with Stripe, Kickstarter's payment processor. You will only get a 1099-K if you exceed $20,000 in gross sales and more than 200 transactions.

Taxes can take up a big chunk of your profits from the crowdfunding campaign. To help the tax laws work in your favor, I'd recommend carefully keeping track of all expenses related to the Kickstarter project. The majority of crowdfunding campaigns on Kickstarter and Indiegogo do not turn a tremendous profit. This means that you can offset the income from the sale of goods/services via reward tiers that we talked about above with business expenses to lower your overall taxable income.

If you're looking to get inside of the mind of a creator that has grappled with this issue, I recommend Glenn Fleishman's article "Pay Caesar His Due." He comes at the issue of taxes and expenses related to crowdfunding campaigns very practically. According to Flieshman, "States that have gross business taxes, like Washington, calculate tax on the amount charged before Kickstarter's fee and credit-card fees." You need to research how your state calculates gross business taxes. In addition, I think this particular segment of his story is incredible important. Listen up. Flieshman continues by saying, "Because crowdfunding campaigns can take months or even years to fulfill, if you launch a campaign late in a year, all the revenue comes in late in the year and is taxable in that year, whereas expenses come in the next year or even a subsequent one for big projects."

Flieshman goes on to say, "You see the problem. In our case, we raised over $56,000 in 2013 (before subtracting Kickstarter and credit-card fees), and nearly all of that money was for services that would be rendered in 2014, such as printing. Because we would eventually incur those expenses, they would offset our taxable income in 2014 — but we still needed to pay the tax for 2013! That can cause a cash crunch if you haven't planned for it."

Overall, I would be sure to keep an extremely detailed excel spreadsheet with all the expenses you've accrued related to the campaign from the beginning to shipping out the last reward. I'd also back up these entries with receipts and any proof of purchase screenshots/PDFs that you can get your hands on to cover your bases.

Now that you're aware of the taxes that you'll face from running a successful campaign, let's go into some of the other costs that you'll experience. Remember, many of your reward tiers will include physical perks that need to be shipped to backers around the world. The goal with all cost estimation is to separate fixed costs from variable costs and to eliminate as much uncertainty as possible going forward. I consider fixed costs to be those that will not change throughout the duration of the campaign and after the campaign. I would lump pre-campaign activities into the fixed category, because you know the definite costs and can factor those into your fundraising goal and the price tags for your rewards.

Examples of fixed costs include:

- Video production.

- Graphic design or artwork used in the campaign.

- Website creation (domain name, hosting, theme).

- Advertising. It can be tempting to increase advertising if the pledges are coming in quickly, but if you priced your rewards so that 5% of the price tag would be devoted to advertising, then don't exceed this margin.

I consider variable costs to be those that may change throughout the duration of the campaign or when the campaign is finished.

Examples of variable costs include:

- Manufacturing. It may seem like getting a quote from a manufacturer ensures that all manufacturing related costs are fixed, but unfortunately, this is not the case. Not only may the manufacturer's pricing structure fall through, but the parts you get may be defective or not up to par. Be safe and get multiple quotes from different manufacturers and research the background and history of each provider.

- Shipping. Depending on where your backers are located around the world, shipping prices may vary.

- Labor. If you attract more backers than anticipated, you may need help packaging and shipping out rewards. The more you raise, likely the longer it will take. You may have planned to fulfill the rewards yourself initially, but if your orders went through the roof, you may need assistance.

It's important to keep the differences between fixed and variable costs in mind because sometimes hidden costs or changes in pricing can sneak up on you, making reward production require more funds than you initially anticipated. I've seen creators that have had to dip into their own savings in order produce all of their rewards, which is the last thing you want to have to do.

Since you'll be experiencing some variable costs, I think that it's important to create a margin of safety. The vast majority of all-or-nothing crowdfunding campaigns don't make huge profits. They'll put in 8-10% in profit. One simple mistake in estimating costs for your Kickstarter can easily chew up this margin. Therefore, I usually recommend that campaigners budget in an 8-10% cushion for their campaign to counteract possible variable cost changes. If everything goes as planned, then there will be a bit of profit from the campaign. If not, then you won't need to dig into your own savings account to finance reward production.

I've been asked time and time again from readers as to how to reduce costs for an upcoming Kickstarter campaign. Basically, the more that you can do yourself, the better. In the next few sections, I'll talk about how you can put together a pitch video cheaply and how to make a nice-looking campaign page on a budget. At the same time, your time also has a cost, along with the time of the labor you hire. You might crunch the numbers and find out that it makes more sense to go with a trusted fulfillment center, rather than doing all of the reward fulfillment yourself. Right now, you're ahead of 90%+ of creators out there on Kickstarter. Pat yourself on the back! Many creators fail to consider crowdfunding costs and don't do any kind of in-depth preparation activity before they launch their campaign.

Lesson #5: Design Attractive Perks or Rewards

Before doing anything, take a second to read through the types of rewards that are prohibited on Kickstarter. You can check out that list in chapter 1, or on the Kickstarter website. Once you've looked through this list, it's time to get started brainstorming some rewards or perks that you can offer backers of your crowdfunding campaign. Kickstarter rewards have three functions.

First, they involve your backers in the creative process. As David Iaituri said, who raised $194,682 on Kickstarter, the real secret of Kickstarter is the community. David went to extra lengths to involve backers in his project, from posting images of the orders being shipped out, to naming product parts after his early supporters. He likened running a successful Kickstarter campaign to how restaurant goers love to watch Japanese Hibatchi chefs cook. The food and atmosphere must be worth the money spent, but it's also about seeing a performance.

The best way to build a community around your project or your cause is to involve backers in the creative process. The goal is to instill a sense of ownership in the project, meaning that community members have a say as to how the project will turn out. Giving backers a way to impact the creative process is great strategy to excite evangelists that will share your project on their Facebook or Twitter. When a backer can directly impact the outcome of the project, be it choosing product colors, adding a line of dialogue to your screenplay, or naming a character in your novel, they will be more emotionally invested in the outcome of the project. They'll also look forward to your updates and be more likely to engage in your mini-community through the comments section (where they will meet like-minded backers who interested in the same type of projects).

The marketing guru and bestselling author Seth Godin has a great quote about pricing, saying that "Not adding value is the same as taking it away." Rewards also provide an incentive for people to back your project. When you ask people to financially contribute to your campaign in return for nothing or a cheap reward (pencils, keychains, etc), you are either asking for charity or effectively cheating them out of their hard earned dollars. Neither situation is a great selling proposition. The most attractive rewards offer some kind of value to the backer at a reasonable price. This value could be physical (the product), creative (input in the project), experiential (the creator will perform an activity, perhaps for entertainment), sentimental (great perk aimed at friends/family as a show of their support), or exclusivity (early-adopter perk).

When you're coming up with rewards, it's likely that your first ideas won't be the best. Set aside an hour to fill up an entire page with reward ideas, and don't be afraid to come up with crazy or silly ones that you think your backers might like. After you've finished, ask a friend or potential backer who is interested in your project to pick out the top 5 that they like most and why. It will give you an idea of the types of perks that your community might find interesting. Don't forget to include pricing to get feedback on this variable also. You must put yourself in the mindset of a backer and try to imagine whether or not you could get excited about the perk for the given price. It might take a while to come up with compelling rewards, but keep brainstorming, and browse through other projects in your category to generate perk ideas. Never create a perk that you yourself would not be interested in as a backer.

To sum it up, there are four main types of rewards.

Experiential: You might promise to do something or organize some kind of cool activity. The goal here is to make an amazing memory for your backers.

Prototype or product: Your backers receive the end product that they supported. It could be the product that will one day be available for public purchase or a limited edition version of the product.

Accessories and enhancements: These are items that add to the positive experience of backing your project. Backers get awesome swag, equipment, or additions to the core product. It's best to have accessories or enhancements that are highly related to the core project.

Involvement: When claiming these rewards, a backer might get to have a character named after them or be able to contribute a line of dialogue.

It's important to come up with exciting reward tiers because when all is said and done, your backers will make or break your Kickstarter project. Roll out the red carpet if you haven't already. Do everything you can to make them feel special up until every reward has been shipped. Keep making updates that highlight the benefits of pledging at a certain reward tier and that encourage backers at lower levels to consider upping their pledge.

Backers will form the heart of your community and be responsible for the bulk of discussion regarding your project on social media networks and the comments section. It's crucial that you deliver a reward tier for these backers that is affordable (not retail price). Remember, once your campaign is done, you will still have permission to email these backers regarding future product offerings and company updates. Generating rapport with all your backers now could lead to greater revenue down the road.

You can also get backers interested in your reward tiers by utilizing the psychological concept of exclusivity. Do you remember a while back hearing about how Hostess, the maker of Twinkies, was going out of business? I don't know about you, but a lot of my friends started stacking up on Twinkies. They went nuts! Why? Because there were only going to be a limited number iconic Twinkies left, and then they'd be gone forever!

Designing a reward tier or version of your product that is exclusive gives lurkers a reason to become backers. There is no longer that excuse: "Oh, I'll get just get one when it's up on their website." Tomorrow, the product will be different and cost more, but today, backers can get in on an exclusive deal to be one of the first owners of your amazing widget. You can also make use of Kickstarter's limited quantity functionality, where backers will only gain access to a particular reward tier while it is still in stock.

I know that I've talked a lot about the importance of coming up with rewards that appeal to your backers, but you have to be wary of one big mistake. You see, many creators that I've spoken with will end up falling into the trap of trying to please everyone. This is the recipe for failure. You're going to get suggestions from friends, family, and target backers to change or alter your reward tiers leading up to the launch of your Kickstarter campaign. Your job is to filter out the good ideas from the bad.

The only thing worse than unattractive rewards are complex rewards. Complex rewards are the source of many fulfillment difficulties. You don't want too many accessories or versions of your product. You're going to have a chance further down the road to offer your product in different colors or styles. Right now, the focus should be on the first version. Make it as easy as possible to bring this new product into the world and get it into the hands of your backers as soon as possible.

This advice extends to any add-ons that you come up with. If you're not familiar, add-ons are not part of the core Kickstarter functionality, but they were created as a way for campaigners to provide more 'rewards' or 'perks' for backers to choose from.

For example, if an inventor is Kickstarting a new phone and wanted to allow backers to also pre-order an accessory for that phone, he or she could offer the accessory as a $15 add-on to an existing reward tier that has already been chosen by backers. A backer, who has already pledged $30 for the phone at the appropriate reward tier, would then need to add $15 to their pledge to claim the additional accessory reward.

To give you a better idea, I've included two snapshots below from the ARKYD: A Space Telescope for Everyone campaign. This campaign raised $1.5 million for 'The first publicly accessible space telescope.'

PLEDGE ADD-ONS

You can add additional items to your pledge level by simply choosing the item(s) you would like and then following the instructions below to add to your pledge! *All add-ons require base pledge to be at the $25 tier and above. Instructions for adding add-ons can be found below:*

ADD-ON INSTRUCTIONS: To add an add-on to your pledge, follow these steps:

- **1) Press the 'Manage Your Pledge' Button above.** If you have not pledged yet, it will say 'Back this Project'.
- **2) Increase your pledge in the 'Pledge Amount' box by the total of the add-ons you want to add.**
- **3) After the end of the Kickstarter campaign you will receive a survey** that will ask you questions so that you can explain how you would like the add-on money assigned.

So, if you claimed the $25 reward for a "Digital SPACE SELFIE" early on in the campaign, but realized later that you would also like a t-shirt, you could select that additional perk as an add-on. As a creator, you must go through a few steps before announcing a special add-on to your backers.

First, you must decide which pledge tiers can quality for the add-on. In the example above, only individuals who had chosen at least the $25 reward tier could access the add-on.

Second, you must price the add-ons appropriately. Don't forget to include shipping and an estimated delivery date. I would also specify the quantity for each add-on. For example, $10 + $3 international shipping = 1 t-shirt (est. delivery date of March 2015).

Third, it's extremely important that you create a long-form set of instructions as to how your backers can go about claiming an add-on and what add-ons are available. I recommend checking out the way the ARKYD: A Space Telescope for Everyone campaign created a landing page with comprehensive guidelines and information about the available add-ons for their project.

Lastly, you can announce the add-on to your backers. I'd recommend announcing it on social media, in a specific update, on your blog, and to your mailing list. You should also include a special note at the end of your rewards section (both the tiers and the section in the campaign text), explaining that there are add-ons available. If any of your backers asked about add-ons, it would also be a good time to respond to those comments saying that they can now check out the add-ons in your campaign text.

Another way that you can increase the pledges to your Kickstarter campaign is to plan to release stretch goals! As I described previously, when you launch a Kickstarter campaign, you must set a fundraising goal, which should reflect the minimum amount of money that you need to bring the project to life. If you hit that target before the campaign's duration runs out, then you will be able to keep the funds that have been pledged by backers, and proceed to fulfill the promised rewards. If you don't hit your goal, none of the backer's credit cards will be charged.

However, what happens if you hit your crowdfunding goal when there is still time left before your campaign ends? This is where stretch goals come in. To give you an example of what stretch goals are, I've included a screenshot below of the "Notion: Be home, even when you're not" Kickstarter campaign.

notion

Be home, even
when you're not.

1,202
backers

$248,792
pledged of $50,000 goal

46   INITIAL
hours to go   GOAL

Back This Project
$1 minimum pledge

This project will be funded on Thu, Oct
16 2014 11:54 AM EDT.

Share 2,091   Tweet   <> Embed

Project by
notion Loop Labs, Inc.
Denver, CO

If the $250k stretch goal is reached for this campaign, then backers will have the ability to own a limited edition color version of Notion. As you can see, you can use stretch goals to motivate your audience to continue to spread the word about your campaign, even after you've hit your goal. Stretch goals will also incentivize new backers to join your project and encourage existing backers to up their contribution amount.

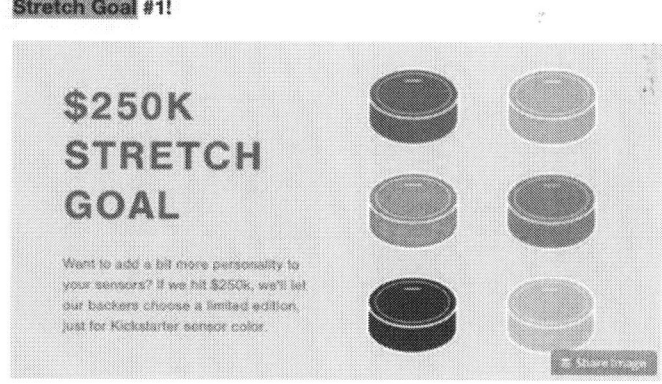

Stretch Goal #1!

$250K
STRETCH
GOAL

Want to add a bit more personality to your sensors? If we hit $250k, we'll let our backers choose a limited edition, just for Kickstarter sensor color.

Help vote on the limited edition color by leaving a comment for us or sending an email to Hello@Notion.is. The color can be anything you'd like to see!

Voting ends 24 hours after we reach our stretch goal.

Usually, stretch goals are enhancements to your project that will be "unlocked" if you hit certain milestones. While not always, these enhancements are often given to everyone who has pledged to the project and claimed a 'perk' or 'reward.' An example of a stretch goal might be that if the project hits 200% funded, then each backer will get access to an exclusive part of the video game or a bonus track on your album. You can advertise perks or enhancements that will be unlocked if a project gets a certain number of social shares on Facebook or a certain number of backers.

Sounds great, right? But, you still have to finance this extra product that you're offering your audience. All successful Kickstarter campaigns must spend a portion of their funds raised producing rewards that were promised to backers. For this reason, many creators don't make a large profit from their campaign. If you are going to add stretch goals to a campaign, then you need to consider whether or not you can finance them.

It's best to choose enhancements that are low-cost to produce or that don't cost anything to produce (aside from a time investment) to minimize the chance that you will be put in the red from trying to make a great experience for your backers. If you are going to offer a significant upgrade, then plan carefully.

Kickstarter warns that "Stretch goals, on the other hand, trade long-term risk for a short-term gain. Tread carefully. What should a creator do if their project is funded with significant time on the clock? The same thing every creator should do: make an unforgettable experience for their backers. Use updates to share the creative process as it happens. Make a connection that goes beyond funding. Money gets spent, but a strong community will last forever."

To help you as you go about crafting your reward tiers, I've included a list of a few items that I've brainstormed.

Games

1. Early access to "Cheats" or bonus levels, characters, abilities, and items.

2. Design your own item, level, or character. Do voiceover for a character.

3. Desktop or facebook wallpaper, poster, soundtrack, or action figure relating to the game.

4. VIP Forum Badge, Early access to future games (or ability to test them before launch), Q&A hangout or Reddit AMA.

5. Hidden section where you can see your name in the game, in the box, or inside the product.

Film + Video

1. Desktop or facebook wallpaper, poster, or soundtrack. Autographed (by team) images or pictures from film.

2. Character from the movie saying a message of your choosing. Character named after backer. Backer can send a prop to be included in the movie.

3. Bloopers, behind the scenes footage, alternative endings, conversations with the actor/director about making the film. Q&A with director or AMA.

4. Be an extra in the movie. Opportunity to have your own script looked over by a professional if you are an aspiring screenwriter. Access to the script.

5. Can take a prop from the movie. Can write one short scene or alternative ending that the cast must act out.

Music

1. Early access to the first single of the album, lyrics, song notes, music video etc.

2. Name in liner notes. Credit on album cover. Signed CD.

3. Artist or band will sing a cover of your choosing.

4. Poster, Desktop art, Facebook cover art.

5. Invitation to concert. Live webcam jam session with band. Include your vocals or bass in new song you create with the band or artist. Invitation to remix tracks and be tweeted out or mentioned on facebook.

Technology & Design

1. Backer will have the opportunity to provide a testimonial after using the product that will be included on the website, used in interviews done by the founders, a blog post that the company writes, etc.

2. Have your name engraved on the exterior or interior of device like the Macintosh.

3. Q&A, AMA, or interview with the founders.

4. Related accessories for the device to expand on functionality.

5. Color, size, attribute variations of the device.

Publishing

1. Name a character after a backer or have a backer name a setting or chapter.

2. Access to exclusive content including drafts, alternative endings, characters left out, plot twists considered, etc.

3. Signed copy of the work, posters or artwork, invitation to write a book review that will be tweeted out.

4. First copy of the audio edition of the book. Invitation to include a testimonial that will be included in the book.

5. Q&A or one-on-one with author to learn more about their intentions regarding the storyline, characters, etc.

This list should give you a few ideas as to what you can offer as a perk or reward in exchange for backing your Kickstarter campaign. Next, I'm going to be covering how to create an effective video for your campaign that gets people excited about becoming a backer.

Lesson #6: Make a Video that Converts

It's no secret. Your Kickstarter pitch video is the most important component of your campaign. It's the first thing that backers see when they visit your page and it's your one chance to make a good impression. Will they be ecstatic, raving, and share your project with all their friends, or will they click off after the first 30 seconds and see what their friends are up to on Facebook?

By Indiegogo's estimates, projects with a video can raise 115% more than projects that do not have a video. According to Kickstarter, projects with videos succeed at a much higher rate than those without (50% vs. 30%). In addition, MWPDigitaMmedia, who analyzed 7,196 Kickstarter projects in 2013, found that projects with a video are 85% more likely to achieve their funding goal. Finally, Professor Ethan Mollick of the University of Pennsylvania examined a Kickstarter data set comprised of 47,000 projects from May 3, 2009 to August 1, 2012 and concluded that an average film project (holding all else constant) with a video would have a 37% chance of success and only a 15% chance of success without a video. You get the message. A video is crucial for your campaign's success.

Before you get overwhelmed, let me say that you don't have to re-invent the wheel. Research is the first step that you should take, whether it's developing a marketing strategy or the storyboard layout of your video pitch. There are so many different types of categories on Kickstarter that blanket advice is not always the best advice. Set aside an hour and create an excel spreadsheet of 10-20 campaigns in your category or projects that are going after a similar backer demographic as yours, and compare.

What elements did their videos focus on? Were there any major differences between the projects that were successful and those that did not meet their goal? What did you find engaging about the videos and when did you begin to tune-out?

In addition to taking note of the structural elements of the videos, I would also pay attention to the emotions that you feel as you watch the videos and which scenes made you feel those emotions. You can use those as a blueprint when attempting to evoke similar emotions in your backers.

At the end of the day, the name of the game is attention. It's your job to maintain the interest and attention of your backers, so that they'll actually listen to your pitch. If you've ever watched SharkTank, you know that pitching is tough! One thing you will notice if you watch that show is that the camera doesn't focus solely on the entrepreneur or the product. Every 20-30 seconds minimum, there is a transition and frequently multiple camera angles.

This is because focusing the camera in the same position for a full 2-5 minutes is boring! By incorporating multiple camera angles or at the very least, transitions, you can maintain your backers' attention and interest throughout the pitch. If you don't believe me, just take a look at popular YouTubers like Philip Defranco or Jenna Marbles. They use jump cuts and transitions throughout their video to maintain attention all the time.

Another way to keep viewers tuned into your message is to use background music to accentuate your major points. Many videos that you'll come across online will feature some kind of light, positive, and upbeat background music. Not only do these positive emotions translate to the viewer and put them in a good mood, but they also help to engender trust. We naturally trust people if we feel positive around them. That feeling of positivity causes us to like them more, and be more likely to listen to what they have to say. These tactics shouldn't be used in a manipulative way, but if you truly believe in your product, they can be a powerful way to evoke emotions towards that product in potential backers.

You can also increase the "trust" and "liking" factor surrounding your campaign by adding humor into your pitch video. We naturally want to share funny videos with our friends. Since the video made us laugh, we hope it will make them laugh. It's a form a virtual empathy and emotional connection. If your pitch video is genuinely funny, one of your backers might want to share the campaign with a friend and say something like "This is hilarious you must check it out." If the video is funny, it will also increase the amount of time that they'll stick around until the end. Why? Because there is a promised future emotional reward! Funny YouTube compilation videos can be long and still rack up thousands and thousands of views. People are willing to watch long videos if they are enjoying themselves.

I think that the term conversion is a bit abstract, and in some ways, mysterious. All it means is that you're converting someone from a browser into a supportive backer. In order to ensure that this happens, you must take the time to not only deliver your message on camera, but also deliver it in the right way. There should be no incongruence between what you're saying and how you're saying it, or how you're coming off in the video. This is why good lighting is so important. Don't just throw a video up on Kickstarter and hope for pledges. People respond to faces. We buy from people that we know, like, and trust. If your image is blurry or if poor lighting makes it difficult to see your face, it's going to be harder to build a relationship with potential backers. People are going to either tune out, not take you seriously, or feel like your claims are sketchy.

Along with having good lighting in your actual video, I'd recommend giving some thought to the thumbnail that you want people to see before they actually click on your campaign and watch your video. YouTube creators have mastered the art of the thumbnail. They figured out how to get rapid browsers between the ages of 18-34 to click on and watch their videos by using intriguing images that capture people's attention. Your crowdfunding video thumbnail not only shows up on websites that embed your video pitch, but it also appears in the Kickstarter or Indiegogo discovery engine. Use this functionality as another way to engage with potential backers. You can even change your thumbnail throughout the duration of your campaign to announce key milestones.

Finally, before I get into the nuts and bolts of putting together a pitch video, I have to mention copyright law. There's no other way to say it. Don't violate it. While the chances seem slim, it's important to be aware of other creator's rights, one of which is the right to take action against copyright infringement. Even if you attribute images/sound/video to the proper source, you can still get in trouble if you do not have the creator's express permission to use their intellectual property. There are plenty of websites that you can use to get royalty free stock video footage or free images that you can use under the creative commons or public domain license.

This is embarrassing, but I was actually threatened to be sued for copyright infringement once. I took an ordinary-looking image off of google. It was nothing special. A lot of other blogs had used it. It was just a picture of money. I could have taken a better photo with my iPhone (and I should have). Long story short, as the blog post that I used it in got more and more popular, I was contacted by a lawyer who represented the creator of the image, demanding payment. After consulting several lawyers, the creator actually did have a case and I was forced to shell out about $1,500. I didn't use the image in a malicious way. I hadn't been able to find the original source of the image. I was even 100% happy to credit the creator, but that's not what he wanted. Use this as a lesson! Don't infringe on copyrights when creating your campaign. If your campaign does well, you could have a lawsuit on your hands.

Now, if you've already started doing research in preparation for your crowdfunding campaign, you'll know that the sweet spot is 3-5 minutes for the pitch video. At the same time, I get people saying all the time, "Well this project had an 8-minute video and they were successful!" The key is that you don't want the viewer to be bored at any time throughout your video or think to themselves "when is this going to be over?"

For most readers, shorter is better. It will force you to weed out extraneous information and focus on making those 3-5 minutes amazing. However, if you have a fan base that you know will watch whatever length video you put up, the 8 minutes are extremely entertaining, and the viewer walks away thinking "That was awesome!" then go for it.

I know that 3 minutes sounds like a short duration, but in internet time, it's super long. 3 minutes is a century. If you don't believe me, you can get a feel for a good video duration by looking through several campaigns in your category. While you're watching their pitch videos, ask yourself:

- Do you begin to get bored at any point?

- When does your attention span wane?

- At what point in the video do they introduce themselves and the product?

- What information do they leave out, but include in the campaign description?

When you finish your video, you should also show it to family, friends, and ideally a stranger or two to get their feedback on its length. In your overall pitch, you should mention:

- Who – Who are you? Why are you credible? What is your background?

- What – What is the prototype or product? Show, tell, and paint a picture as to how someone would use it in their daily life.

- Where – Where will this product be made and what regions can you ship it to?

- When – When will the rewards ship out or when do you plan to complete the project?

- Why – Why are you doing this project? Why are you passionate about it? Why is it needed?

- How – How are you going to execute on your vision for the project?

Remember, the video is meant as a teaser, a pitch, or a trailer that will introduce you, the product, and why it matters. Backers can always look through your campaign text for more information. I don't think you need to hit all of the above points in the video, as you can explain them in the campaign text, but I do think there are some crucial ones that you should cover.

If you do nothing else, tell a story. Stories are an integral part of the human experience and a good story will even captivate strangers, as we saw with the Esinton Glass Kickstarter campaign, which raised nearly $200,000 (Episode #13 of Crowdfunding Demystified Podcast). Ask yourself, why did your team or you create the product? This will help backers get to know you, your values, and get them excited about your solution. The SolarPuff Kickstarter campaign, which raised nearly $500,000 had an amazing inspiring reason as to why they decided to create a eco-friendly lantern (EP #29 of CD).

You should also ask yourself, wow are your backers a part of this journey? Why are you bringing this project to a crowdfunding website and what will your backers enable you to do? The Makesmith CNC Router video, which raised $80,000+, clearly explained why they were raising money through crowdfunding (EP #14).

You can bring credibility to your project with a killer video that stands out. For example, you can use your video to show your viewers the impact that your product/initiative is having. This could mean featuring multiple people in your video or highlighting testimonial reviews like the Greenbelly Kickstarter campaign, which raised 190% of their goal (EP #21).

Finally, each video should have a clear call to action. Give your backers a reason to pledge to your project. Don't just ask for money! Ask them to join you on a quest. Invite them to become a part of your community. Challenge them to change the world with you. What is your call to action? Call to actions get a bad rep from gimmicky marketers using phrases like "Don't wait to buy now!" and "Limited time offer, get it while it's hot!" The true underlying purpose of a call to action is to focus someone's attention on what action they should take now that they have watched your video, visited your website, or read your blog post. If you are speaking to a particular audience, think about how the items in your project will resonate.

Should they support the project to bring back a previous game series you made?

Are they pledging their hard-earned dollars because getting your product out there will change the world?

Ultimately, your call to action should connect the problem that the potential backer is experiencing or cares about with your solution and how they can make it possible.

Although there have been some successful crowdfunding projects that have commercial-style videos, I think they are the minority. Your project video should not be an impersonal commercial for a product. If this all sounds confusing, a good way to think about a great crowdfunding pitch video is to compare a regular commercial to an apple commercial. Have you seen how Apple creates videos about their latest products? They describe the effort that went into making it and what the mission was behind the product. It's clear they deeply care about their products and have put a lot of thought into the design.

At the end of the day, the video must be a narrative. I think Rob Balder who raised $130,688 on Kickstarter said it best:

"Narrative is the story you tell about who you are and what you want to do. You have to convince potential donors of several things. First, that you are a person worth supporting. Second, that this idea is worth making real. And finally, that you are a person who is capable of coming through and actually making it come true."

Of course, if you have the budget and don't want to take the time to create and edit the video yourself, you could consider hiring a professional. If you don't have the budget, there are alternatives! In my interview with TagTalk, I learned how the founders employed local university film students to help create the video. It was a great learning experience for the students and an inexpensive way to make the video.

"We emailed local universities that carry film programs. Usually the departments are proactive about getting students some hand-ons experience, so they broadcasted about the task and helped us to schedule two meetings in a very short timeframe.

We met an avid film practitioner the very next day who had access to all the filming equipment needed, loved our idea, and who lives just down the street!"

If you decide to film your own pitch video, first, take into the account the information that I've already given you in this chapter. Look at other videos in your category that have done well, and those that haven't. If you're still unsure of a good video format, I'd split your video in the following way.

10% humorous or entertaining.

40% on the pitch and problem/solution.

30% showing your personality (passion, story, approachability, etc).

10% bringing credibility to the project.

10% the direct sales pitch.

When I first started helping creators with their campaigns, I was surprised to discover that there are specific types of emotions that are commonly associated with viral content.

- Viral videos tend to evoke:

- Curiosity

- Amazement

- Astonishment

I don't know about you, but I've definitely shared at least one video on my friend's Facebook page saying, "Oh my god, this is sooo cool!"

We tend to share posts and images on Facebook that:

- Resonate with our identity. No wonder why we share so many personality quizzes.

- That evoke an emotion in us. We then want to give a friend that same feeling. That emotion could be anger, awe, or amazement. We want to spread that emotion or find empathy.

Keep in mind that you might not be able to appeal to all of these emotions in your Kickstarter video. However, I would pinpoint what you want potential backers to feel after they watch your video pitch.

They might feel angry about a cause you highlighted and want to help.

They might get inspired about how your product can change their life.

They might be so entertained by your game that they can't help buying into the project, because they want to play the game when the full version comes out!

Finally, they might feel a sense of awe or amazement. It could be the design, functionality, or mission that evokes that feeling. That's when they'll say to all their friends "this is so cool!"

Below, I'll include a few resources that you can use to improve your video pitch.

Free Video Editing Software

Video editing software makes it easy to create a professional pitch. Most programs are simple enough for inexperienced users to learn, and advanced options are available for those who are more experienced. Here are a few video editing programs that I recommend trying out.

Lightworks: This is a good free video editing tool if you are going after control. This advanced software takes a while to get used to, but its features, effects and smart trimming tools are so great, "the program has regularly been used to help produce top Hollywood movies such as Mission Impossible and Batman."

iMovie: Great if you have a mac and relatively easy to get started.

Kate's Video Toolkit: Good if you don't have a lot of complex editing to do and don't want to spend a lot of time learning how it works. Kate's Video Toolkit comes with a file format conversion tool, allows you to trim and join videos as well as add a soundtrack.

Windows Movie Maker: Easy to use and supports most file formats. Adding special effects, transitions, sound tracks, credits, etc. is simple. There are other functions like trimming clips, and you can save the file when you're done or want to publish it to a website (like YouTube or Facebook).

Avidemux: This is a small open source video editor that allows you to apply a lot of useful filters such as removing noise, adding a logo, and changing brightness. Avidemux offers many fine-tuning options but takes a bit longer to learn.

VSDC Free Video Editor This is a non-linear video editor that may take more effort to learn but has a lot of useful features: drawing and selection tools, sound effects, color and lighting correctors, etc. You can also optimize your video for mobile devices.

Sites for Stock Videos

Using stock videos can save you time and money. Instead of shooting your own video (especially if you don't have the equipment or expertise), there are a wide variety of stock videos online – just remember to credit your sources when necessary. Here are a few sites for stock videos that I recommend checking out.

Shutterstock: Easy to use and has a large amount of stock videos to choose from. It is affordable, with prices based on video resolution.

Pond5: "Open marketplace for buyers and sellers of royalty-free clips in all categories." Users can upload and price their own videos so there are many high quality videos at affordable prices, starting from $5. It has a simple system for previewing videos.

Fotosearch: "The company sells royalty-free and rights-managed photography, illustrations, video footage, clipart, and audio clips." This site offers rights managed and royalty free stock video.

Videohive: Allows users to upload and price their own content. It offers a large amount of footage, allowing you to choose between a regular license (for videos that aren't for sale) and an extended one (that allows you to sell the product after).

Royalty Free Music Sites

Another way to spice up your crowdfunding videos is to include music. Many websites offer royalty free music in a variety of genres. Here are several royalty-free music sites I recommend!

Incompetech: Offers a wide range of royalty free music. The site categorizes music by both genre and feel, making it easy to find what you need. All they ask is that you credit the site in your video.

Free Soundtrack Music: Royalty free music (and paid options) that can be easily downloaded for use in any type of video, film, or game.

ccMixter: A music site that offers soundtracks under the Creative Commons License. Some music may require that you credit them in your video. The site allows you to listen, sample, and mix music.

You can also consider approaching users on SoundCloud or BandCamp to see if they would be willing to let you use their songs in exchange for a credit or mention.

Sites for Stock Photos

Another way you can save time putting together your crowdfunding video is to get professional quality images from stock photo sites.

Pixabay: Free stock photos! We use these photos for a lot of our blog posts on CrowdCrux, a blog about crowdfunding.

FreeImages: The "Leading Source of Free Stock Photos."

Veer: Offers millions of images including royalty-free stock photos and fonts. It also has a design and creative focused community, allowing you to interact with like-minded people.

Where to Hire an Actor

Hiring a voice or video actor doesn't have to be expensive! If you're on a shoestring budget, you can consider Fiverr, which offers a wide range of affordable business services.

Some of these include graphics and design, writing and translation, video and animation, advertising, etc. In the Commercials section you can find many specialized options for as little as $5, with examples like, "I will create a promotional video featuring twins!" and "I will create a 60 seconds High Quality Explainer Video in HD for $5".

You can also try the Craigslist jobs section in your local area to find a cheap video presenter or voice-over actor.

Lesson #7: Craft Compelling Copywriting

Copywriting is very different from traditional writing. It breaks many of the rules that you were taught in high school about what "good writing" is. The reason that it breaks so many of those rules is because you're not writing for an academic scholar. You're not writing a dry business email. Your audience is the average person, who comes across your campaign on Facebook or through your email list. Coming from that perspective, you should maximize for ease of readability, language that conveys confidence, and words that evoke emotions. You're selling a product, team, or story.

Your crowdfunding campaign page is a sales letter. If you make it right, your campaign text will get visitors excited about your project and turn lurkers into backers. First I'll cover some of the basics of putting together a great crowdfunding campaign page. Then I'll get to the techniques that you can use to make yours stand out.

The first thing I'll say is that it's crucial you use headlines appropriately. There's a reason that textbooks, newspaper articles, blogs, and magazines use headlines to separate blocks of text. It makes it much easier to scan through the content and pick out sections that are relevant to you. It seems like a no-brainer, but many campaigns I see read like long essays. Make it easy for people to go through the elements of the pitch, with descriptive and eye-catching titles. You don't want them to see long blocks of text and quickly close the browser window. If possible, create images to serve as the headlines. These will stand out much better than simple text.

You should also break up your text with short and point-driven paragraphs. Ideally, the first sentence of every paragraph should encompass the primary point you are trying to make. Each sentence following the first sentence should support or elaborate on this point. When you are finished with this point and would like to introduce a new topic (or expand on your topic with supporting points), a new paragraph should be created.

For example, this sentence and new paragraph would be a supporter to my previous paragraph and by making it a new block of text, it's easier on the eyes and makes the pitch much more scannable.

Don't be afraid to use bolding, links, and italics. You might not think it, but when people are scanning an article or pitch, their eyes really do gravitate towards bolded words, links, and italics. Use these tools to convey tone or emotion in your pitch.

You can also accentuate your points by adding images in between the paragraphs of text. As stated previously, long blocks of text aren't just bad organization, but they really turn people off from whatever it is you are trying to communicate. Simply put, they are confusing and intimidating. Don't give your readers a reason right off the bat to close their browser window! Break up your paragraphs with relevant images and illustrations.

If I had to boil down all beginner mistakes to one thing, it's that often times, new entrepreneurs come from a "professionalism" mindset and writing style, having spent most of their life in corporations. On Kickstarter, emotion and passion trumps "professionalism."

For example, in English class, we were taught this erroneous idea that it's wrong to use "I" when writing for a reader. We were also taught that terse, sterile sentences convey professionalism, and are therefore best. While it's true that for some audiences, extreme formal writing is required, the goal when launching a crowdfunding project should be to empathize and connect with potential backers.

Backers love intense passion. In a big-business social media driven world, individuals want to connect with other individuals more than ever. The companies and people who win out are the ones that can establish rapport or genuine one-to-many relationships with their customer base. Don't write like you are a corporation. Write like you're a human being. Show your backers how passionate you are. Share your vision.

At the same time, you must put the backer first. If you are using the words "me," "I," "mine," etc, you should only be doing it 10-20% of the time. During the rest of the time, the focus should be on your visitors.

How does the campaign benefit your backers?

How will their life become awesome because of this product?

Why will their contribution make this project a reality and ultimately change the world for the better?

"When dealing with people, let us remember we are not dealing with creatures of logic. We are dealing with creatures of emotion, creatures bristling with prejudices and motivated by pride and vanity." - Dale Carnegie

If you want a shortcut to good writing, simply use definite, specific, and concrete language. Definite and concrete language is much better than abstract or general descriptions.

"He grinned as he pocketed the coin," is better than "He showed satisfaction as he took possession of his well-earned reward."

You can also use the active voice to come off with more confidence in your pitch.

"Dead leaves covered the ground," is better than "There were a great number of dead leaves lying on the ground."

"Amy loves Steve," is better than "Steve is loved by Amy."

It's easy for me to say that you should incorporate this and that into your writing, but it's hard to actually do it. One way to catch yourself before you fall into some of these pitfalls is to read your pitch out loud

Writing is just another form of communication. Your goal when composing a crowdfunding pitch should be to communicate your vision and idea to another human being. There's no worse way to keep yourself at a distance than to use stilted language or incorrect grammar. Read your entire pitch out loud.

Are you using language and grammar that you would use if you were speaking to someone in person?

By reading the pitch out loud, you'll catch awkward sentences and places where you need to be clearer with what you're trying to say.

I know that these are a lot of different tips for improving the actual text of your campaign page. It might all be a bit confusing. Let's simplify it a bit. Your campaign page should include the following:

- Answer the who, what, when, where, why, and how points that I outlined in the pitch video section.

- Use images with text for headlines or major points.

- Use images (and gifs if possible) to showcase the product, team, and your story up until this point.

- Underscore why your team is credible. Include any media mentions or awards.

- Have an FAQ section. Update it as you get comments and questions.

- Supplementary video if needed.

- Hyperlink images appropriately. If the image is of a picture of a reward tier, hyperlink it to the pledge button so that it's easier for backers to pledge.

- Have a basic fulfillment timeline and project schedule.

- One call to action towards the end of the campaign (image that encourages visitors to back this project or share it).

- Don't forget that your title, description, and thumbnail are the first things that visitors are going to use to get a sense of what your project is about.

Finally, try not to think about the money when you're crafting your pitch. It will put you in the wrong mindset. You should be striving to sell the project as an experience. Don't think about how you will benefit from this crowdfunding "transaction." I've sold enough products and started enough businesses in the past to know that if you begin with thinking about how a relationship will benefit you, you are bound to fail. I've made this mistake more than anyone else. You need to start from the beginning with how this project or opportunity will benefit someone else.

Why is this an awesome experience that they want to be a part of? How can you create such a great product that they'll want to tell their friends about it? You can bet that people who backed the Pebble Watch or the Ouya told their friends about it!

At the end of the day, you are not fostering a transaction where money passes from one party to another. You are trying to build a community around your project, mission, and possibly, life goal.

Lesson #8: Communicate Effectively With Your Backers

One of the little-known ugly truths about running a crowdfunding campaign is that it doesn't always go as planned. In fact, I can almost guarantee you that something unexpected is going to happen throughout the course of your Kickstarter project.

Maybe there are delays when dealing with the manufacturer after you've been successfully funded. You might find out that your backers really want you to offer a particular reward, but that it would mess up your entire budget. Heck, something terrible could happen, which makes it impossible to fulfill the rewards that you've promised hundreds or thousands of backers.

The good news is that frequent Kickstarter backers are familiar with delays and unexpected events. Supporting a crowdfunding campaign is a far more raw and uncertain transaction than purchasing a product from an ecommerce store. But, there is a specific protocol that they'll expect should you run into any mishaps. There is a right way to communicate appreciation, updates, bad news, and rally backers at the close of your campaign, when they only have hours left to get in their pledge!

First of all, you must always be transparent. Always. Transparency means updating your backers, should troubles arise. Transparency means clearly explaining the risks involved with your project. Being "transparent" is another way of saying that honesty is always the best policy, with regards to your team, abilities, expected fulfillment date, and anything that you promise to your supporters.

As a precaution, I always recommend that creators set low and realistic expectations, so that it will be easy to exceed them. Don't promise what you can't deliver. I won't name any names, but I've seen several projects get funded early, promise certain stretch goals or add-ons, and find themselves unable to meet those promises.

You should also set a regular communication frequency. The longer that you go without communicating to backers, customers, or investors, the more likely they are to fill the big mystery boxes with answers of their own. They'll begin to raise questions like:

"Is this project a scam?"

"Does the creator really care?"

"If he's busy working on the product, why is he posting on ____."

"Why haven't I gotten my reward yet! I want a refund."

You don't want to give your backers the option of even briefly thinking about the worst-case scenario. Not only does it damage the relationship that you've built up with them, but one might get little antsy, post on a message board, and it will hurt your brand. Regular communication, even if it's basic and simply serving as an update, will set minds at ease and reassure backers that your project is on track.

While your project is live, regular communication is the most basic way to keep your project at the forefront of each person's mind, which makes it more likely that they'll mention your campaign at a party, while out for drinks, or share the actual page on Facebook.

However, before you begin sending out any emails, updates, or social media messages, you should first pinpoint how you want backers to feel about you and your campaign. If you were backing a Kickstarter project, how would you want to feel? Here's how I'd want to feel:

- Like my opinion is heard and taken into account.

- The creator cares about the project and is working hard to deliver on his promises.

- I'm part of something big. A cool new project that's going to change the world, even in a small way.

- I will get the vision I bought into and a copy of the product.

- I'll be able to brag to friends and celebrate the success of the project.

Your expectations may differ when you support a Kickstarter project, like one of the creators on our forum, but these are mine. If I didn't feel like my opinion was being heard, I might try to get heard by posting on a message board, writing a blogger, contacting Kickstarter, or posting a frustrated tweet. If the end product wasn't what I signed up to support, I might ask for a refund or get angry if the creator hasn't acknowledged that fact.

Once you determine how backers want to feel, it will be easier to set the bar for how they should feel about crowdfunding and your project in general. For example, if you know that your product is half-baked and there is the possibility of slightly altering the product before it gets in the hands of your backers, then set that expectation going in, so that they aren't surprised and angry further down the road.

Any incongruence between how a backer wants to feel during the process and how they actually feel as news or updates come to light can be softened with good communication, honesty, and transparency. When it comes to backer relations, emotion trumps information. Always be thinking about what emotion you're conveying with a particular update, comment, or email. Are you coming across as begging, desperate, or annoyed? Or are you coming from a place of enthusiasm, optimism, humility, and respect?

Often times, forgetting to be mindful of how we sound can come back to haunt us later down the road when future backers or customers bring up our Kickstarter page and look through the previous comments we've made or updates we've written. Each time you communicate with a backer is an opportunity to convey information and associate a particular feeling with you or your brand. This is exactly why you should never get in a public or private argument with a backer.

Getting an argument serves no purpose, whatsoever, other than to stroke your ego if you "win" and alienate the other person if they "lose." Arguments online are also magnified when other backers read what you've written, which sours the community as a whole.

As a rule of thumb, be polite, humble, and compassionate. Just because a backer or customer brings up a concern, doesn't mean that they are the only ones who have that concern. Likely, others do also, they just haven't said anything yet.

Finally, communication is all about relationship building. If I had to sum it up in a formula, a relationship = personality + promises. I don't know about you, but I was always taught by professors and employers that you should always conduct yourself in a professional manner, write formally, and take life and business very seriously.

When it comes to indie creation and online marketing, this couldn't be further from the truth. People connect with people, not brands or products, especially if it's their first time purchasing from a new business. The best way to build up your Karma or credibility online is to simply make good on your promises.

The second way is to interject a bit of your own personality into the mix, which will make it easier to develop a positive relationship with your backers. They will get a sense of who you are and what you're about.

Here are a few fun ways that you can show your personality:

- Make an inside joke. This works best if all of your backers share the same profession or interests.

- Reference and comment a neutral current event.

- Write in a conversational tone (read your text out loud) and use idioms.

- Tell a compelling or funny story.

- Share a relevant personal fact about yourself.

Part of building a relationship with a community is making sure that individuals feel heard, part of something larger than themselves, and that there is a camaraderie with other members who are enthusiastic about something similar, like 3D printing or graphic novels.

Shout outs can also be used to highlight community members who have gone above and beyond to help your project, shine your spotlight on happy backers, or deal with ongoing concerns.

Overall, you shouldn't make the majority of an update, comment, or email about yourself or your personality, but one or two sentences can help bridge the gap between you and these strangers that have discovered you online.

I know that we've been talking a lot about feelings and emotions. At the end of the day, the only thing that matters is whether or not you're progressing in business. Are you getting more backers? Are you growing your sales? The way to ground all of this communication in reality is to tie every message to a specific call to action. Simply put, a call to action tells your backer what to do next after reading your update, watching a video, or seeing your email.

You have their attention, now what do you want them to do? Leave a comment? Choose an add-on? Up their pledge to a higher tier? Share your project?

Call to action messages are frequently used in marketing and are also an important part of converting website visitors into Kickstarter backers or, after your campaign is successful, to direct visitors to a particular website.

The chief currency online is not money. It's not even eyeballs, followers, or backers. It's relationships and credibility.

"It takes 20 years to build a reputation and five minutes to ruin it. If you think about that, you'll do things differently." – Warren Buffett

In a world where everyone has a voice, a positive message can spread like wildfire, be shared on Facebook, and go viral. A negative message can do the same, and hang around for years to come.

In this chapter, we've covered the major pillars that go into creating a robust Kickstarter campaign. Next, I'll be diving into some of the marketing strategies, tricks, and hacks that most successful Kickstarter projects use to gather a crowd, raise money, and get written about by major media outlets.

Chapter 5: Marketing Your Kickstarter Campaign

Occasionally I'll see a campaign raise a bunch of money on Kickstarter with absolutely zero marketing. Either the gadget is innovative, the product really scratches an itch, or people find it to be hilarious. These types of campaigns are the outliers, not the norm. Most campaigns, are launched with a powerful marketing plan, even when the creator already has an audience.

When I mention the word "marketing," usually the word "promotion" also comes to mind. Marketing is much more than simple promotion. It also includes the images that you choose to include in the campaign pitch, and the subtle psychological techniques that you use to get visitors to take action.

In this chapter, I'll be walking you through the entire marketing engine that powers a massively successful Kickstarter campaign. Each element is designed to turn browsers into backers. Let's get started.

Rule #1: Your Email List is King.

Your email list is the Holy Grail of all of your marketing activity. Everything that I mention in this chapter should be used to build your email list leading up to the launch of your Kickstarter campaign. Why is email so important? According to Mckinsey & Company, "Email conversion rates are three times higher than social media, with a 17% higher value in the conversion."

The individuals who sign up for your email list are not simply numbers. They're not just random people around the world that make up an abstract statistic. They are real human beings with thoughts, feelings, desires, and emotions.

Despite the rise of social media platforms like Pinterest, Instagram, Snapchat, Facebook, and Twitter, email is still the #1 marketing channel out there for getting regular and new Kickstarter backers to take action. Think of email as the "home-base" where most backers receive information about the topics that they care about.

Tomorrow, Facebook could change their algorithm so that no one sees your posts. Your website could be hacked. You could find that your Instagram profile is banned for some reason. But, you'll always have your email list. If you have 1,000 people subscribed to your email list, then 1,000 individuals have raised their hand saying, "I want to receive messages from your company." Think of a room with 1,000 people in it. That would be a massive crowd!

The reason that email is so powerful is because it allows you to direct traffic to a ***designated place*** at a ***specific*** time. You don't have to wait for people to see your messages on social media, which might be drowned out by all their other social media messages. Instead, they can all check out your crowdfunding campaign at the same time and back it! This is why many campaigns see so much activity and so many pledges during the first day of their launch, which usually spills over into the next two days.

Now that you know the importance of an email list for boosting pledges to your Kickstarter campaign, you're probably wondering how you can actually get email subscribers. Before we get into that, you need to choose an email list provider to manage all of these emails that you'll be collecting. I know that money is tight, which is why you're planning on launching a crowdfunding campaign in the first place! However, it would be a huge mistake to not use an established email list management provider, like MailChimp, which is free up until 2,000 subscribers, or Aweber, which has been around for a while and has great functionality.

Why do you need one of these tools? Simple. Robust email software will:

- Give you analytics every time you send an email marketing campaign. You'll see the number of people who click links, open that email, unsubscribe, and more.

- Let you create auto-responder sequences that begin every time someone opts into your email list. You can use a sequence of automated messages to direct subscribers to a webpage or convey a message.

- Make it super easy to set up a series of pre-scheduled email messages, which can be a great way to automate some of the marketing process as you lead up to the launch of your campaign.

- See who opens your emails most frequently.

There are many strategies that you can use to get more email subscribers. The first strategy that I'll be discussing is the concept of a "lead magnet." A lead magnet is something valuable that you can offer website visitors that will make them want to hand over their email address in exchange for access to the lead magnet. Think of it as a small bribe. Your website visitors should find this lead magnet to be useful, entertaining or valuable. Before giving them free access to this content or opportunity, you'll be asking for their name and email address. This will allow you to market to them in the future. Essentially, they are opting in for more messages from your company.

For example, at the time of writing, KickstarterForum.org is a free lead magnet. In order to register for the forum, you must enter your name, email, and other details. When you register, you are then allowed to ask questions, interact with other users, and promote your Kickstarter campaign. You also get access to special promos and giveaways on the forum.

I am providing value in exchange for your email address. This gives me the privilege to send you marketing messages in the future regarding new books, products, or services that I create that I believe will help you raise more money on Kickstarter and further your business goals. At any time, you can choose to opt-out of my emails.

When you offer a website visitor something exclusive or beneficial, he or she will be more likely to subscribe to your email list, because they will get something out of the relationship. If you're looking for examples of other types of lead magnets, you could use MailChimp to direct the subscriber to:

- A behind-the-scenes special video.

- Deliver an exclusive invite to a Kickstarter launch party.

- Send them a link to a poll or secret FB group where they can vote on something related to your organization.

- Get an exclusive discount code that will give them 10% off of the products or services of partner companies.

- View an awesome hilarious company video "beware: don't watch this video for our upcoming fundraising campaign while you are at work, or you will burst out laughing."

Think of these value-adding ideas as mini rewards that are meant to gain the interest of a potential subscriber so that they are more comfortable handing over their email address. You are building a relationship with them before you introduce them to a paid product.

If you're having trouble coming up with a lead magnet, I'd recommend looking into how your visitor discovered your website in the first place. It could have been through social media, a search engine, an article you've written, or an event you attended. Pinpointing the source of the traffic will help you figure out the type of content that you should offer them in exchange for subscribing to your email list. For example, if someone discovered your website from an inspirational video that you posted on social media, which will be a part of a larger online awareness mission, then it's likely that they'd love to receive more content like this!

You can use resources to help track this information like:

- Google analytics.

- Bitly links.

- CrazyEgg heat map and click tracking.

- Mouseflow mouse tracking.

Once you have an idea of what you're going to offer as the "lead magnet," it's time to set up the functionality to actually collect an email address. If you have already set up an email opt-in form on your website, ask yourself three questions:

- Where is the email opt-in form on your website?

- What is the first thing that should draw a visitor's attention when they visit your site?

- Why did a visitor come to your website in the first place?

Now, ask these questions to a series of visitors that you've connected with (friends, family, individuals who are interested in your project). You might know where your email opt-in form is, but do they? You might want to direct their attention to a particular video, link, or email opt-in form the moment that they visit your website, but what actually is grabbing their attention?

In the simplest form, you can just have a link on your website that visitors click to subscribe to your email list. You could even just have a button. You can also use tools to capture email opt-ins like:

- OptinSkin (for Wordpress)

- OptinMonster (Wordpress)

- SumoMe

- MailChimp's Evil Popup Mode

Once you implement opt-in functionality on your website, you will probably see a small jump in subscribers, but, it's not enough action in the long run. You also need a strong call to action. You must consistently ask your visitors to subscribe. This might seem silly, but you'd be surprised the amount of email subscribers that websites lose out on simply because they forget to ask a visitor to subscribe!

One way to put this in perspective is to watch YouTubers who have millions of subscribers and who have made a living out of making online videos. What's the last thing that they say at the end of every video? It's something along the lines of "if you enjoyed this video, take a moment to give it a thumbs up or leave a comment." They might also say "subscribe if you'd like more funny prank videos like this!"

The golden rule is to always be selling. Always be highlighting why people should subscribe, particularly if they've taken the time to watch one of your videos, read through a blog post, or go visit your website. Don't just tell people what you want, which is to subscribe to your email list. Explain to them why it's awesome for them if they subscribe.

Aside from adding an email opt-in to your website, you can also create a landing page to direct visitors to your email list. A landing page is very different from a full-blown website, which has all of the information about your team, your mission, and your journey. The purpose of a landing page is to solely to collect an email address or have your visitor take an action, rather than exposing them to lots of information about your company or project.

You might set the landing page as your homepage leading up to the launch of your crowdfunding campaign, or even have a custom domain name that you reference should you attend any conventions, do interviews, or get linked to by a media publication.

A great landing page will share compelling information about your upcoming project in an organized fashion, through text, video, and images. It will also highlight the benefits of participating in your upcoming your launch.

You can use tools to help you build this landing page, like:

- LaunchRock

- Unbounce

- LeadPages

- OptimizePress (if using WordPress – more complex).

- Free: Use WordPress and a landing page theme.

I've highlighted a few tools and techniques to get more email list subscribers in anticipation of your crowdfunding campaign launch. Ultimately, the only way to get more subscribers is to drive traffic to your website or landing page and adjust the positioning/wording of the call-to-action messaging that you're using to get a visitor to subscribe to your email list. This means that you need to use trial and error to figure out the type of incentive that gets a visitor most excited about signing up for your email list. You'll need to adopt this same mindset when putting out content to get people on to your website.

Rule #2: Keep Your Email List Engaged

From the time that someone gets on your email list to the second you launch, you are building and strengthening your relationship with that person. In my interview with John Lee Dumas, an award winning podcaster and millionaire entrepreneur, he described how he built an email list of thousands of subscribers over the course of a year. But, he didn't just let that email list go cold. He continued to engage with these subscribers.

By sharing his story, giving subscribers a glimpse into the making of The Freedom Journal, and teasing the upcoming Kickstarter campaign, he built anticipation, improved his credibility, and ultimately, was able to raise $453,803 from 7,063 backers.

You can't expect to just convert a cold email list into sales. You must first warm them up to the product, who you are, and why they should care. If you're an advanced marketer, I would recommend segmenting your email list to get the most out of your subscribers. You could announce your campaign first to the subscribers that are most likely to become backers, and then to the rest of your subscribers to capitalize on the social proof created with the initial core group of subscribers. I'll discuss social proof in a later chapter.

Rule #3: Start Growing Your Social Media Profiles

I can already see the collective eye roll. You're a creative type, or an entrepreneur! You don't want to deal with social media. Shouldn't people just follow you, because you're awesome? Believe me, by investing some time and learning how to build up followers on your social media accounts, you'll increase your future success exponentially. When you launch on Kickstarter or Indiegogo, you'll have a bunch of interested individuals with whom you can share your new campaign!

I define the main social media networks as:

- **Facebook.** Facebook is one of the largest social media networks out there with 1.71 billion monthly active users in 2016. Key trends are mobile adoption, video consumption on Facebook, and the changing Facebook algorithm.

- **LinkedIn.** LinkedIn is the largest professional social network with 450 million members. The platform has grown a lot in the last few years, with the introduction of articles and content on the website.

- **Instagram.** While I don't think Instagram is as mature as Facebook with paid marketing tools, it's still a very powerful network to gain followers and get people interested in your cause.

- **Twitter.** Finally, many have argued that Twitter is a waning social network, but I don't agree. There are still a large number of people who get their news from Twitter and check it daily.

You could also look into networks like SnapChat and Pinterest, but I wouldn't include these in the main list. Ultimately, you'll probably narrow in on one or two of these social networks in the long-run. My Twitter is certainly much stronger than my Instagram. You'll find the network that is the best fit for your organization, but you should have a presence on all of them!

Now that we've outlined most of the major networks, you're probably wondering...how are you actually going to get followers? How are you going to get people to take time out of their day to follow you and receive messages related to your company?

You won't be using social media to share thoughts like "My cat just rolled over." You will be using social media as a tool to figure out what type of content your audience likes and what causes they care about.

As a rudimentary example, let's say you are trying to start a business that sells a cool new product for people into health and fitness. You decided to share a post on Facebook of a before and after photo that was sent in by a customer. Maybe it also has an inspirational caption. You also link to your Kickstarter campaign. Now, if this photo got lots of clicks and shares, that tells you that potential backers are moved by images like these. You should share more inspirational images in the future.

You may even consider creating similar content on your company's blog. In the long-term, it would attract readers to the blog, who are also part of your customer base. You will then have the opportunity to ask them to pledge to your upcoming crowdfunding campaign.

Basically, there are two words that sum up why people will follow you: content marketing.

You're going to be putting out content that will either be informative/useful or entertaining. This could be content that you create or content that you find on the web. Informative content could take the form of articles, tips, ideas, and advice that you share to help them achieve their goals in some way. Entertaining content could take the form of quotes, images, shocking or inspiring facts, etc. This type of content is emotional. People will follow you based on how they perceive you will make them feel in the future. You may make them feel inspired, motivated, or hungry to reach their goals.

By continually putting out free content that resonates, you'll begin to build an audience on these different social media platforms. Yes, this takes time. Accumulating followers and improving audience engagement doesn't happen overnight. If you're just getting started, plan for this to be an eight month to a year-long process before you begin getting some momentum. In that span of time, you will figure out what types of content works best for your audience, when the best time to post is, which social media channels are a good fit for your company, and you will gain an in-depth understanding of the problems that your customers care about.

Eventually, you'll start to mix in your own "call to action" messages on social media, like asking people to back your crowdfunding campaign. But, you shouldn't start here. The primary focus should be to get people to follow your social media profile, so that they'll get notified when more content comes out.

After hearing this strategy, you might be thinking, "This sounds like a lot of work. How am I going to find time to do all of this?"

I've used this simple strategy to build up thousands of followers on Instagram, Facebook, and Twitter. I agree, it does get difficult to keep up with all that work! That's why I've automated most of my social media marketing.

Thankfully, when it comes to social media marketing, there are lots of tools out there that will allow you to pre-schedule social media messages that will go out in the future. I'm horrible at being consistent. Even my tennis coach used to say, "Sal, you need to be more consistent with your swing!" These tools let you sit down and spend two hours planning out all the social media messages that will be shared on your Facebook page for the next month. Then, you don't have to worry about it for the rest of the month.

I'd recommend looking into:

Hootsuite: A powerful social tool to save time managing multiple social networks. If you haven't heard of it, it's a tool that you can use to schedule Tweets and Facebook posts ahead of time on your phone or on your computer.

Buffer: Buffer is a Hootsuite competitor that lets you manage your Twitter, Facebook, and LinkedIn social profiles. Buffer makes it super easy to share any page you're reading. Keep your Buffer topped up, and it will automagically share your various messages on social channels through the day

The great thing about these two tools is that they also come with analytical capabilities. I personally use Buffer, which tells me how many people are clicking on the links in my social posts, sharing them, and which posts are seeing the most engagement. I can also re-schedule posts to go out.

By putting out engaging content, networking with users, and automating the entire process with one of the above tools, you can be sure that you'll begin to see more and more users following you online. This process works for every social network out there!

As you begin to gain more and more followers, you'll be building a small army that you can leverage once you launch your upcoming Kickstarter campaign. These followers will also give social proof to your campaign and put you head and shoulders above creators who don't have any kind of social media presence. Finally, you can use social media to build your email list, which should be the primary in-house sales channel for your product or project. By directing followers to your website or a landing page, you're sure to see a boost in signups. More relevant email subscribers will translate into more backers.

Rule #4: Get Free Traffic From The Media!

Believe it or not, but you can get the media to send free traffic to your Kickstarter campaign. This is why I love PR and media outreach. When a journalist decides to write about you, you'll not only gain credibility in the eyes of your backers, but you'll also gain access to all of the readers that love and trust that media publication. This entire process might seem mysterious, but journalists are just like you and me. They are busy creating value for their customers, which are readers and advertisers. They can be influenced to write about certain topics, if it will bring in more traffic and advertising dollars.

There are two ways main to influence a journalist. You can either get their attention with a press release or direct outreach. Most beginning Kickstarter campaigners have never written a press release, so I'm first going to cover what to include in a press release and how to craft a compelling story. Then, I'll talk about direct outreach and go through some of the techniques I've discovered to get the media to write about you. Finally, I'll share a few press release tools out there that you can use to automate and simplify the entire process.

The first thing that you must take into account when drafting a press release for your crowdfunding campaign, is that crowdfunding differs from many other traditional product launches. There are a few elements that every Kickstarter campaign has in common, which I'll break down below.

Fundraising Duration: Every Kickstarter campaign has a set fundraising duration, which will impact the amount of time that you have to take advantage of any PR attention or media hits. Therefore, you need to be super organized when drafting a PR outreach strategy. Some media publications will offer the "embargo" option if they like your project and want to write about it. Basically, this means that they will hold off on the publication of the article until a certain date.

Rewards and Perks: The rewards and perks offered throughout a crowdfunding campaign are a great way to incentivize lurkers to become backers. Some of your backers might care about the mission of your project. Some might connect with you, or find your video engaging. Others will simply want to learn about what kinds of perks you're offering. Make sure to include these in your press release. Also, by underscoring the "limited" or "scarce" nature of your perks, you'll get more people to check out your campaign.

Social Proof: Backers are more skeptical than ever! Unfortunately, a growing number of campaigns have defrauded backers or have simply not fulfilled on their promises. Therefore, any way that you can add social proof or credibility to the campaign will make it more likely that journalists will check out the project or that potential backers will. Social proof can include the number of social shares, backers, comments, or dollars given. Credibility can include media mentions, partner organizations, or simply a compelling founder story.

In addition to these elements, there are a few other items that you should keep in mind when creating the PR draft for the launch of your crowdfunding campaign.

Do you have an eye-catching headline? In the same way that click-bait news headlines give readers a reason to click through to the story, you want to have an interesting headline for your press release and the subject of your email so that a journalist has a reason to read further.

Have you included images or multimedia? Words are one way to tell a story. Images and video are other ways to get a story across very quickly in this social media driven and attention-starved world. Make sure you have high resolution images on hand that the journalist or blogger can use in their article. Often times, the number of images or multimedia you can send is limited, so provide a link where they can find more multimedia assets.

Are there quotes from the founder or team? Have you ever noticed how news or human interest stories tend to include quotes from reputable sources? They might even quote the founder themselves, if it's a new startup company. Rather than making the journalist call you up for an interesting quote, include that quote in your press release! You can also include testimonials from backers or partners to add to the social proof of the pitch.

Is it easy to find relevant links and contact information? I can't tell you the number of times that I've been emailed asking to cover a story and the email didn't have a link to the company's website or the URL of where I can find the campaign. Make it as easy as possible for journalists to find where your campaign exists online. They might be on their mobile phone and not want to search around to find it.

Have you answered the who, what, when, where, why and how? It's true that the press release should spin an enthralling story and make the journalist envision how awesome of a story this would make for their readers. However, it also needs to include concrete facts, like when the campaign will end (or start), what the product is, who designed it, and why they are so passionate about this project.

How hard is it to read the press release? It's always best to put yourself in the shoes of someone reading the press release. Is the information easily digestible? Are the paragraphs short and to the point? Are you using active verbs and strong grammar? One easy way to get an idea of how well it's written is to read it out loud! You'll quickly catch any grammar or spelling errors. You'll also get an idea of how the sentences flow.

What emotions do you arouse in the reader? Finally, a press release is part art and part science. Ask a friend who is familiar with your industry to read your press release and analyze how they feel after having read the story behind the crowdfunding effort. Are they excited to learn more? Bored? Are they confused? Simple questions like these will give you an idea of the tweaks you might need to make to elicit the desired emotional response.

You can also get journalists interested in your press release by fitting your story into the overall media environment. Identify how your crowdfunding campaign relates to hot topics and trends that journalists and bloggers are currently writing about. For example, right now, teaching coding in inner-city schools is gaining traction. There are niche blogs writing about programming, education, and STEM. There are also larger publications creating content about the technology industry.

If you created a crowdfunding campaign to help educate kids about coding, you may want to consider contacting publications that have written about these topics, as you are a prime example of a growing trend and therefore newsworthy.

Again, how does your story fit into the overall global discussion? What trends are you a part of? Research the publications engaged in these trends.

The other thing that I'll say before I share how to go about contacting journalists is that you must appeal to multiple audiences. Is your Kickstarter campaign for a new tech product that will have a big impact on a particular industry? What organizations will benefit down the road if your campaign raises the needed funds?

For example, when Arnold Schwarzenegger was working to attract media attention for his breakout film Conan the Barbarian, he appealed to multiple audiences in order to get the ink needed to fill theaters.

"To promote the movie, it was important to work every possible angle. We used special-interest magazines to build an audience – stories on sword fighting for the martial-arts magazines. Stories for horse magazines. Stories for swords and sorcery. Stories for bodybuilding magazines on how you needed top conditioning to be Conan." – Total Recall: My Unbelievably True Life Story

Let's start to talk about how you can directly contact journalists and get them to write about your crowdfunding campaign. Email is still the preferred method of contact, but I've also seen campaigners get media stories by contacting journalists via Twitter and LinkedIn.

How do you stand out from the crowd? According to a survey conducted by BuzzSumo, Journalists receive 25-100 pitches via email per day and countless more on social media. In order to stand out, it's best to avoid cliché buzzwords and stick to a succinct, straight-forward, and relevant pitch

Be succinct. Get to the point, and if needed, use bullet-points to highlight the major reasons why this news is important and a good fit for the publication. Don't write an essay. Your email should be scannable.

Be straight-forward. Avoid PR buzzwords that only serve to make it more difficult to understand your story and why it's a good fit for the publication. Otherwise, you will sound like all the other companies pitching the journalist and fail to stand out.

Be relevant. Why this journalist, why your company, and why does this story matter now? Don't just copy and paste generic emails. Tailor your pitch to both the reporter and the publication.

When is the best time to pitch a reporter? After conducting several informal interviews, PrDaily put together an awesome breakdown of the best time(s) to reach out to a journalist. Overwhelmingly, all of the reporters surveyed preferred to be pitched via email in the early morning. However, due to the large volume of weekend mail, the participants also suggested to wait until Tuesday, once the Monday rush was over and they had more time to look over each email.

This information is corroborated by MarketConsensus, who also recommended sending pitch emails between 8 am – 11 am and to avoid Mondays.

Should you send mass emails and if so, when? Despite the overwhelming industry advice not to send mass emails, I've actually seen responses from them and I've gotten stories as a result of them. Many journalists may not like these practices, but they can work if you have a killer headline, pitch, and are going after a bunch of publications with a similar audience.

However, I do think they should be used in conjunction with direct pitching and relationship building. That being said, if you're going to send out a mass email with services like PRWeb, MyPrGenie, PRNewswire, SBWire, or others, then take into account the best time to send that email. **S**ubscribers' top engagement times are 8 a.m. – 10 a.m. and 3 p.m. – 4 p.m. with up to 6.8% average open rates and CTR (click through rate).

PR goes to experts in their space Sometimes when you're marketing a new fundraising effort, it's easy to forget that you're in "this" for the long haul, whether that's growing your company or starting a new one.

In my experience, experts in their space will never have to worry about getting PR. What was the first thing that happened on TV when Malaysia Airlines Flight 370 disappeared? The media brought aviation experts on to comment about the event and the implications.

Experts are cited in the media all the time! Even I was quoted in a recent CNN interview. The important thing is to put yourself out there as an expert, so that you can seize these opportunities for some free PR. How can you frame yourself as an expert in your space and use that as an angle for a story, or to get some free PR indirectly? HARO is a great free resource for these types of PR hits.

87% of Reporters love data, facts, and figures. Have you ever noticed when a "new study" is released that analyzes data points to corroborate or highlight an interesting trend, it goes viral on news outlets? How can you enhance your pitch with facts, figures, and data? How does your company fit into a larger cultural trend?

Backing up your vision and story with numbers is a great way to snag attention away from other pitchers, just pushing their "game changing" initiative.

P.S. Just kidding about the 87%

Journalists must write about things they don't want to. I'll tell you a little secret. Journalists don't necessarily want to write about every story, but sometimes they have to.

You're really going to tell me that if a holiday is coming around, like Christmas, that a publication isn't going to look for Christmas stories? Or if a particular story is blowing up like the Potato Salad Kickstarter, an editor isn't going to say "I want this story on my desk by _____."

Newspapers are in the business of attracting eyeballs and advertisement dollars. Most major publications always need to write about what is trending, or they'll be left out of the flow of online and mobile traffic.

The question is: How can you fit yourself into the stories that are trending. You need to begin to think about what kinds of stories reporters will be looking for given the time of the year and what's happening in the current media discussion.

Repeat business = success. There is a big difference between a Kickstarter project that has repeat backers and one-time backers. The same is true for PR. Rather than seeking one-time transactional relationships, it's best to develop a long-term relationship with a journalist. They may move publications in the future, and you'll be able to continue to get PR hits. They might also forward you along to his or her friends, who are also journalists.

You should take a long-term view of PR outreach. This is exactly what a PR agency does, and they are in the business of getting their clients stories. Why wouldn't you take the same approach as a professional PR firm?

A relationship with even a handful of reporters can yield dividends down the road. Go out of your way to be helpful to them. Connect them with sources or people in your industry they'd like to speak with.

Your email headline must be clickable. It's hard to have a clickable headline without knowing your audience, which brings us back to point #1 (relevancy). Ideally, your headline should be tailored to the individual reporter or publication.

Your name and headline are the first few things a reporter is going to see when they look at your email. How can you phrase the headline to get them interested in learning more?

One technique I've found to be helpful is to see if there are any headline commonalities in other articles that have been published by that reporter and then craft your email subject to be similar to those headlines.

There is no blueprint. Although there are "best practices" and mistakes to avoid, getting PR is a learning process. You need to figure out what works well for your company and your industry, which will take time.

Personally, I've had experiences that fly in the face of the common industry advice in terms of the ideal times to send emails and how to best do journalist outreach. Keep in mind that these are general guidelines, and they are not set in stone.

I think the most worthwhile takeaway you should get from this section is that you need to adopt a PR mindset. You need to begin to observe the news, TV, and print media and begin to form questions. Why did a publication quote this expert, or why did this reporter choose to write about this particular story? Beginning to make yourself aware of the inner-workings of the news media will help you begin to become active on the pitching side. To help get you started, I've put together a list of different press release websites that you can check out.

Press Release Websites:

- CrowdfundingPr.org
- PRLog (free)
- Free Press Release (free)
- 188PressRelease (free)
- 24-7 Press Release (free)
- Pr.com (free)
- i-NewsWire (paid)
- PrWeb (paid)

- PrNewswire (paid)

- BusinessWire (paid)

In this chapter, you discovered a few surefire ways to market your upcoming crowdfunding campaign, along with a few key tools that you can use to make the process much easier. These techniques will only work if you take action and actually implement them! You have to start now. You'll thank me later! Start building your email list, social media profiles, and start developing a relationship with journalists. Next, I'm going to dive into some of the psychological hacks that you can employ to get more backers and raise funds for your upcoming Kickstarter campaign.

Chapter 6: Mastering Backer Psychology

The media gives the impression that business is all about dry numbers and calculation. While analytics and data are immensely helpful, what's even more useful for boosting your sales is actually quite rare. It's empathy, plain and simple. The more that you can empathize with the emotions that your target customers are feeling, the better. You can then amplify the emotions that lead to buying your product or backing your campaign.

In this chapter, we'll discuss some ways that you can employ Jedi Mind Tricks to stand out above all the other crowdfunding campaigns out there, gain credibility, enhance the trustworthiness of your company, and get website visitors to take action!

Rule #1: Social Proof Creates Trust and Lowers Defensive Barriers

I'm a pretty normal young man living in NYC. I don't smell, I'm reasonably intelligent, and I'm told I have a nice smile.

But, if I were to go up to a random person on the street and say "Hi, nice day, right?" more often than not, I'd get looks of confusion, suspicion, annoyance, and many people would nervously smile and rush past.

I know this because I actually do this sometimes just to work on my social skills and face social fear.

People are naturally suspicious in our culture of strangers and organizations that we haven't heard of before. It's because the person **suspects** that the other person wants something from them, which puts them on the defensive and raises their guard.

There is no familiarity, trust, or value in the interaction. Also, everyone else is on their way to work or another destination, so it feels "weird" for them to respond to or stop and talk to a complete stranger. It's an interruption.

Social proof is one way to jump this barrier and gain instant trust. Here's how Wikipedia defines it:

"Social proof, also known as informational social influence, is a psychological phenomenon where people assume the actions of others in an attempt to reflect correct behavior for a given situation. This effect is prominent in ambiguous social situations where people are unable to determine the appropriate mode of behavior, and is driven by the assumption that surrounding people possess more knowledge about the situation."

When a product or individual has social proof, others will approach them from a perspective of **curiosity** rather than skepticism. They're more likely to take a second to watch your video or read your fundraising page because "other people think it's interesting, so I might as well check it out."

It's basically thinking that just because a book is bestselling that it's probably good and worth buying. You might even take less time to check it out than a non-bestselling book.

If you've ever seen a bunch of people surrounding one person in a group setting, I'm willing to bet you thought, "Is that a celebrity?" or you were more apt to go and join the crowd yourself to see who they were.

Social proof evokes curiosity. When you lead with social proof, rather than being skeptical, the prospective backer is more likely to focus on the mission, story, or awesome impact that your company has had. They'll be intrigued instead of suspicious.

There are a few ways to create social proof, including:

- Testimonials

- Genuine activity and donations

- Comments section

- Media hits/write-ups

- Social sharing

- Reviews/emails

- Credentials and endorsements

While growing vanity metrics like social media followers or the number of visitors to your website shouldn't be your main goal, they can be leveraged to enhance your credibility in the minds of potential backers. This is one way to get visitors to take action. A campaign with high social proof is more likely to convert browsers into backers. Rather than clicking off your page, a visitor is going to open their wallet and put in their credit card information.

The worst thing that could happen is that a visitor comes to your campaign and sees 0 pledges, 0 social shares, and a half-baked "ask." It makes them feel like little real work went into putting together the Kickstarter page. They'll rationalize that either the company isn't serious, that the cause isn't worthy of their funds, or that something else is wrong, because no one else has given money.

On the flip side, if someone discovers your campaign online and sees a bunch of pledges pouring in or massive engagement and social sharing activity, they're more likely to take a sec to watch your video and read through your pitch. The fact that other people are paying attention to the crowdfunding effort makes them want to learn more. It evokes curiosity and engenders a stronger feeling of trust.

Rule #2: A Sense of Urgency is What Prompts Action

The reason that people **take action** is because there's an impending deadline or other event, which creates a sense of urgency.

I don't know about you, but I was definitely one of those kids who procrastinated most of the college semester and then crammed two days before the exam. Many of my nights were spent in the library the day before a final paper was due.

Of course, the best and most *rational* thing to do is to plan, take action according to your plan, and see the desired result. But, most people aren't rational. We're guided by our emotions.

When someone feels a sense of urgency about a particular activity, they will:

- Focus and drone out distractions.

- Take massive action in a small amount of time.

- Overcome hurdles that would normally set them back.

- Pay less attention to hindering emotions or thoughts.

- Look to short-cut signals to make micro decisions.

- Take more risks.

I've written and spoken extensively about how a Kickstarter campaign's fundraising meter will grow and flatten out over time. Many campaigners see an influx of pledges towards the beginning and end of their campaign. Both of these events create a sense of urgency among supporters, whether it's to claim limited quantity "rewards" or get in before the doors close on your campaign.

The best Kickstarter campaigners are able to prompt action throughout the duration of their fundraising campaign. But, the great thing about crowdfunding is that the basic model *encourages* urgency due to the temporal nature of the fundraiser. It's your job, as a campaign manager, to communicate this emotion to your backers, so that they feel this urgency. Don't just assume they'll feel it. Communicate it. Repeatedly.

The more you create a sense of urgency in the minds of your backers and campaign visitors, the better the chance that they'll actually take action and give money to your project. Of course, this is assuming that you put together a great campaign page. Even with a great page, you'll still raise money, but when you effectively communicate urgency, you'll raise even more money.

Rule #3: Build Relationships at Scale

Okay, I get A LOT of emails and many of them start like this…

"Hey Sal. Love the blog and podcast. Tell me, how do I get strangers to back my campaign?"

First of all, I don't do consulting at the moment and always direct people to my FREE online content. I only provide advice if it benefits the community, like on my forums or the comments section. I wish I could provide it one-on-one, but I simply don't have enough hours in the day.

Second of all, you can't get strangers to back your campaign. However, you can turn strangers into FRIENDS and then get them to back your campaign. It's a subtle distinction.

The way you do this is by building relationships at scale.

Here's the idea summed up. Since everyone thinks **you** want something from them, break the pattern by giving them something **they** want. It has to be something they actually want and it has to add value to their life in some way.

As you begin to provide quality content, advice, or free value, the people will begin to feel like they know you. When someone watches a free video that you put together, they'll get a sense of your values, and eventually, they'll develop an emotional connection with you.

This is EXACTLY why we feel like we "know" big-name YouTubers or celebrities and are completely okay shouting out their name in public or buying something they endorse. In fact, I'd go so far as saying that we feel like we "love" certain comedians because we relate with them so much and almost consider them to be a friend.

We're willing to watch a 5 minute video created by a random person in the world if it makes us say "wow," laugh until we cry, or if it resonates with us and inspires us to be a better person. When you put out content in the form of videos, emails, social media posts, blog posts, or images that educate, inspire, or entertain, you're investing in the relationship with your potential backers and customers.

Ultimately, you're doing all of this to simply build relationships with multiple people at once. A thousand people can watch one video on your Facebook page and come away feeling like they know a bit more about you and your company. This is powerful. In the past, you'd have to directly interact one-on-one with the same number of people to create that type of response.

When you do this over a span of time, you can get 1,000 people to subscribe to your email list, or to follow you on a particular social media channel. I know it works, because I've used it to build my own email list to over 20,000 subscribers. I've used these techniques to grow an online forum to over 6,000 users, get over 100 positive iTunes reviews for my podcast, and make a living doing what I love. By the way, I'm a millennial. When I started, I didn't have what older people label as "experience." If a kid can figure this out, so can you. I'm also giving away the formula. You just have to copy it. Remember, all of this is what gives you the leverage that you need to CRUSH IT during the first week of your Kickstarter campaign.

Rule #4: Stories Trump Logic

When is the last time that you sat through a two hour long YouTube video lecture? Probably never (though if you have, that's awesome!). But, people around the world are 100% okay with sitting through a 2-hour movie in a dark room. Even if the movie sucks, they'll stick around because they want to find out what happens.

The same goes for TV shows. How many times have we heard friends say "okay, let's just see what happens and then we'll change the channel." We'll default to this even if it's a trashy show or it isn't good, and we pretty much know what's going to happen.

Stories are powerful for three reasons:

- They create anticipation.

- They hold attention.

- They encourage empathy with the characters and challenges.

If you want someone to feel **exactly** how you felt in a given situation, weave a story around that event. Don't just tell them how you felt.

Quite simply, the best stories **communicate information** and make you **like** or at least feel close to the main character. They are a powerful vehicle for creating trust online.

Not only are they a great way to get people excited about taking action and joining your campaign's community, but they are also super good for seducing journalists and bloggers like me to write about you!

Many of the successful crowdfunding campaigners that I've had on my podcast pitched me with a compelling story, which I then wanted to share with the podcast listeners.

I hate to break it to you, but no one is going to remember the statistics you put out, not even your key customers. Statistics are an important way to establish credibility, but they aren't great for arousing strong emotions. But, I can almost guarantee you that EVERYONE will remember a compelling story. The more emotions that someone feels, the more likely they are to remember an event and also take action in the moment.

You should be sharing your story though several mediums and across multiple platforms. I'm not just talking about the social media platforms out there. I'm also referring to your email list, and when you're speaking at events.

A great story will bring listeners into your world, and when they feel what you feel, they're more likely to take the action that you think "makes complete sense." For most readers out there, that's to contribute the funds to enable a cool product or project to come to life.

Rule #5: Create the Emotion of "Liking"

Okay, I know that I sound like I'm a robot right now. I really do enjoy analyzing emotions with the rational side of my brain. I also must ***strongly emphasize*** that the techniques I'm sharing in this post should only be used if you genuinely believe that you have an amazing product that will make other people's lives better.

In Robert Cialdini's seminal book, Influence, he reveals 3 key points, that I'll highlight below:

- "We like people who are similar to us in terms of opinions, personality traits, background, or lifestyle."

- "Familiarity also plays a role in decisions. Seeing or experiencing something more and becoming familiar with it leads to greater liking."

- "A halo effect occurs when one positive characteristic of a person dominates the way that person is viewed by others. We assign favorable traits to good looking people without logic."

In case you missed kindergarten, when we like someone we are more likely to help them, support them, and take the time to listen to what they have to say.

I'm not saying that you should try to force people to like you or to not be genuine. I'm saying that you should be aware of the emotions that your words, imagery, video, and content creates.

Making a joke in your video might make *you* nervous, but it might make *them* laugh, feel good about themselves, and like you more.

If you're speaking to a group of programmers, you're probably going to generate a great feeling of "liking" if you yourself are also a programmer, can make inside jokes, or relate to the job lifestyle. If you're a business guy who doesn't know the first thing about programming and you assume certain things or butcher key terms, it's unlikely that the audience will see you in a favorable light.

Being focused on how much your backers like you or your team is another great way to avoid typical objections that bog down many Kickstarter campaigns.

For example, a skeptical backer might harp on the negative qualities of online giving with regards to credit card security. Let's be honest though, online security is a reality. This is innovation we're talking about. You then have to deal with that objection.

If that campaign visitor likes you, then they are going to approach the campaign from an entirely different mindset. Maybe instead of focusing on *that* particular aspect, they'll smile at what you're trying to accomplish, decide to support it, and rationalize that you're a good guy so you will be forthright with issues that you or they encounter.

Of course, you should be 100% transparent and forthright with any complications. Just keep in mind that the degree to which someone likes you will affect how they rationalize the things that you ask of them.

To sum it all up, you don't come off as some faceless company with a big board of directors that is just looking to raise money. Personalize it. You want to come off as an actual human being, and in the best case scenario, as a likeable friend.

These key rules form the bedrock of a sound marketing strategy. You should always have them at the back of your mind when you're engaged in backer communications. They're used every day by marketers to sell products to the public. They aren't just for businesses though. You can steal them and apply these techniques to getting visitors to take action and pledge to your Kickstarter campaign. They're proven to influence the only thing that matters, getting your backers to ***take action***.

Chapter 7: Life Post-Kickstarter

These key rules form the bedrock of a sound marketing strategy. You should always have them at the back of your mind when you're engaged in backer communications. They're used every day by marketers to sell products to the public. They aren't just for businesses though. You can steal them and apply these techniques to getting visitors to take action and pledge to your Kickstarter campaign. They're proven to influence the only thing that matters, getting your backers to **take action**.

After you've completed your Kickstarter campaign, the real work begins. You're going to have to ship out all of the perks or rewards to your backers. This is a lot more work than most creators initially think. It takes strong logistic and planning skills. In my opinion, you can only call your Kickstarter campaign a "success" once all of your backers have a reward in their hands. You don't want to become another Kickstarter scam story.

In this chapter, we'll go through a few tools and techniques that you can apply to the Kickstarter fulfillment phase of your campaign. I'll also share some of my own thoughts for turning your Kickstarter success into a thriving business!

Lesson #1: Self-Fulfillment vs. Outsourced Fulfillment

If you are planning a crowdfunding campaign or have recently finished fundraising through Kickstarter or Indiegogo, I'm sure you've come to realize the major financial and time cost of reward or "perk" fulfillment. When you tally up shipping and handling, trips to the post office, stamps, bubble wrap, and time spent stuffing envelopes, fulfilling your backer's rewards can seem like a part-time job. Remember, these are the people who believed in your project and pledged their hard-earned money to see its completion. Expedience is of utmost importance.

Many campaign creators struggle with the question as to when it's appropriate to outsource fulfillment and when they should just stick it out and obtain the help of friends and family. Now is the time to evaluate how much you can commit each day to reward fulfillment. It's also important to develop a timeline explaining how many perks you can fulfill each day and how many days it will take to fulfill all of the orders you expect to or have obtained from your crowdfunding campaign.

If you're working a 9-7 job with commuting, and are also committed to home cooked meals, exercise, and being able to relax in front of the television, it may not be realistic for you to meet your fulfillment goal in a reasonable timeframe. Obviously, weekends are a great way to catch up on work related to your Kickstarter or Indiegogo campaign, but after a long anxiety-ridden week, the last thing most people want to do is take on more work on the weekend.

If you are extremely driven, have a written plan, and know you can deliver in a reasonable timeframe, awesome! But, if you have doubts, have major work-related travel plans, or don't like the idea of committing your weekends to fulfillment, then it might make sense to pass on the stress to another group of individuals. It's true, you will have to sacrifice some of your margins, but think of it as buying peace of mind and buying free time. In addition, the order fulfillment company will likely have experience with international shipping and customs, factors that most people need to spend time researching.

Also, before even considering the possibility of outsourcing fulfillment, it's important to ask: Can you afford it? If your margins are already razor-thin, you may not have much of a choice. Any added costs will bring you into the red. You might not like it, but this is the time to solicit help from friends, family, and neighbors.

Once you've made sure that every backer receives exactly what they pledged for, go back and be sure to look through your financials and do a cost analysis. Are the low margins a result of the crowdfunding medium, or is there a larger element in the equation? Where you can cut costs or get a better supplier rate for improved margins? At some point in time, if you intend to sell the product independently, fulfillment services will likely be necessary and at that time, it will pay off to have better margins so that you can afford it.

If you are doing a one-time project and don't intend to sell your product after having raised money on a Kickstarter or Indiegogo, then you may not need to worry as much about your relationship with service providers and fulfilling more product orders. However, if you are intending to go into business after the completion of the project and continue to sell the product, then establishing a relationship with an order fulfillment center early on can help you negotiate better rates, anticipate costs, understand fulfillment-related problems, and give the company a test-run with a small batch of orders.

Solving the problem of order fulfillment is the first step in building the infrastructure and systems that will help automate your business in the future. If you are using Kickstarter or Indiegogo as a launch pad into starting your own company, I'd recommend getting acquainted early on with order fulfillment companies, as this is a crucial element of your business.

Lesson #2: Avoid The Most Common Fulfillment Problems

Popular crowdfunding platforms like Kickstarter and Indiegogo have attracted tons of creators who want to introduce the world to amazing new products. The problem is, sometimes the features they promise are too good to be true. As a creator, make sure you only promise what you know you can do, instead of having to explain to backers why you can't later.

Examples of far-fetched projects are pretty common, with many of them even being suspended by the platform they launched on before their campaign even ends. Manufacturing issues are what caused Bonaverde to dissolve, a company that launched three crowdfunding campaigns for their roast-grind-brew coffee maker that never made it to backers.

As a general rule, start with something simple that you know you can produce. If your project is really successful and you start growing your capital, you can always test later to see if you can add new features and launch a newer, better version of the product.

In addition, I'd make heavy use of excel spreadsheets as you're going through the fulfillment aspect of your campaign. The costs related to shipping can quickly add up. You must take into account international shipping, domestic shipping, taxes, time-related costs, packaging, postage, and more. What happens if you receive far more demand than you expected and you exceed your fundraising goal? The worst thing that could happen is that you don't allocate enough of your budget to the fulfillment phase of your campaign and you actually end up owing money after all the campaign has finished. Don't make that mistake.

Lesson #3: Get Help If You Need It

There are five different categories of fulfillment software that can make your Kickstarter order fulfillment much easier:

- Inventory Management
- Warehouse Management
- Transportation Management
- Vendor Management
- Labor Management

Of course, if you're new to fulfillment or you're a small start-up without the warehousing and facilities to run your own fulfillment operation, learning to use these solutions can be overwhelming and unnecessary. Don't worry, there are also many all-in-one options available where they do most of the work for you. You just need to choose which one is right for your project.

When deciding between the all-in-one and DIY software options, ask yourself, "Does my team have the expertise to do fulfillment ourselves?" "Will the service pay for itself through increased efficiency and things like cheaper shipping rates?"

Once you make your decision and narrow your preferences down to a few platforms, you'll be ready to start asking for quotes, since most of them are industry and volume specific. I'll highlight a few tools that you can use below.

Amplifier: Amplifier is a one-stop fulfillment solution that lets you integrate your suppliers, use their 90,000 sq. ft. warehouse, ship your goods and they'll even make products for you and help with customer support! Amplifier gives you a convenient way to sell t-shirts, hoodies, totes, posters, mugs, iPhone cases and more without holding inventory. It's perfect for creators who want to offer lower reward tiers in addition to their main ones. Best if all, Amplifier integrates with your favorite ecommerce platforms, like: Shopify, WooCommerce, Bigcommerce, Magento and Gumroad.

Fulfillrite: Fulfillrite is an ecommerce order fulfillment company that prides themselves on offering customers fast shipping, transparent pricing, and dedicated support. They also integrate with many popular ecommerce platforms, including: Magento, Shopify, WooCommerce, Celery, BackerKit, Bigcommerce, eBay, Amazon, and more! One of the great things about Fulfillrite is their passion for helping smaller startups and creators of crowdfunding campaigns figure out fulfillment issues. Some of the other services that Fulfillrite offers are return processing, inventory storage, and T-shirt printing.

BackerKit: BackerKit is one of the most crowdfunding-oriented services on this list. They give you the specific tools you need to deal with all aspects of your Kickstarter campaign, including backer surveys, answering questions, add-ons and pre-orders, customer management, and automated shipping. BackerKit focuses mainly on Games, Design & Tech, and Film & Video projects, with many users stating that BackerKit helped them save time and money during the fulfillment process. You can use code CROWDCRUX for a discount.

Floship: Floship is a global ecommerce platform that is known for its fast and cost-effective worldwide shipping services. They focus in excellence when it comes to hiring the right couriers and integrating with the best ecommerce platforms and order management systems. They also have a conveniently located warehouse in Hong Kong – the world's largest air freight hub.

Acutrak: Acutrack offers complete, on-demand fulfillment solutions. They specialize in producing and fulfilling CD, DVD, USB, and Book rewards. What's great about Acutrack is that there are little to no inventory commitments (unlike some companies that can have large minimum order quantities)! Like any top fulfillment platform, Acutrack lets you integrate with leading ecommerce platforms like Amazon, WooCommerce, 3dcart, Shopify, Bigcommerce, and more. They also have a blog on Kickstarter fulfillment and have worked with crowdfunding campaigns.

Simple Global: Simple Global is another platform that specializes in global ecommerce fulfillment. One of the cool things about Simple Global is that they can save you time by taking over some of your merchandising tasks, making it easier for you to go global by listing and managing your products internationally on your behalf (this includes things like translations and converting currencies). Their staff deals with packaging and shipping in their warehouse, giving you not only an all-in-one solution but also some peace of mind.

Fishbowl: Fishbowl is an inventory management system for QuickBooks. With Fishbowl's software you can automate your manufacturing, avoid stock outs and overstocks, and automatically reorder materials (to name a few features). You can try Fishbowl for free for 14 days. In addition to QuickBooks, Fishbowl integrates with Amazon, eBay, Dropbox, Magento, FedEx, Shopify, UPS, and more. Customers say the program is user friendly and that Fishbowl has very responsive customer service.

Freightview: Freightview's freight management software helps you save time and money on freight shipping by giving you direct rates for all of the carriers and brokers you use. You can look at all of your offers on one website and when you pick one, Freightview schedules the pickup for you. This system also helps with shipping labels, tracking shipments, reports and analytics, and more. Freightview offers a 30-day trial for new users.

Systems Logic Software: Wireless Warehouse in a Box: Wireless Warehouse in a Box is a warehouse management system with 85% mobile capacity, meaning you can accurately keep track of your inventory from the palm of your hand! System Logic Software integrates with QuickBooks and NetSuite, and is recognized for their award winning customer support. System Logic Software's connections give you the tools you need to manage your warehouse as efficiently as possible, including cloud-connected inventory so that you and your customers can always see what's available.

U Route: U Route is an easy to use transportation management system. This web-based SaaS platform helps tighten the connection between shippers and carriers. U Route can make your fulfillment process easier by giving you a way to keep track of your contracted transportation providers and rates in one place. They also provide you with other tools like analytics, bid capabilities and direct e-carrier management. U Route offers a 30-day trial during which they try to prove to customers that they can save them at least 10% of their transportation costs.

Lead Commerce: Lead Commerce offers inventory, warehouse, and order management software all in one place, with an emphasis on small business. Their easy to use web management lets you keep track of customers, warehouses, inventory, and orders and shipping, making your entire business more efficient. Lead Commerce also offers a free trial and has several integrations, including: Square, FedEx, and UPS.

Choosing the right fulfillment solution or tools to use depends entirely on the type of project that you are running. You will have to decide whether your operation is small enough (or you have enough space and experience) to handle fulfillment on your own, or whether you should outsource some, or all of the work.

Lesson #4: Keep Getting Orders After Kickstarter

I've seen this happen more than you might think. A creator launches a campaign and as a result of great marketing or the Kickstarter ecosystem, they begin to see pledges pour in. In fact, as they're nearing the end of their campaign, they're dreading that moment when backers can no longer pledge to their campaign. They've created so much momentum and they want to keep the campaign going!

By its very nature, crowdfunding is temporal. A specific fundraising duration creates urgency, which is a critical reason why crowdfunding works. However, there are ways to capture and continue to build this momentum, even after your Kickstarter campaign has ended. I actually recently got a great email on this very topic from a member of B3 Innovations, a 3d printing hardware company.

"I discovered your podcast a few weeks ago and I have been addicted ever since! I spend a lot of time driving and now I look forward to my commute so I can listen to another episode...

We are working on our second campaign as we speak and definitely learning as much as possible this time around to boost our total funding. I've been noticing a trend, and maybe you have covered this in previous episodes, but I've seen multiple campaigns launch on Kickstarter... AND launch on Indiegogo after they complete Kickstarter. It seems this is a tactic to boost overall funding...Thanks for your contributions to the crowdfunding community."

Let's explore a few ways that you can keep getting orders after your Kickstarter campaign has completed.

Spotlight: Kickstarter's spotlight feature helps creators continue to share their product's story with backers and members of the press after they've successfully completed their campaign. It also allows creators to create a call-to-action button and direct it to a website of their choice. You can customize the color, text, and URL of the button. This means that you can direct website visitors to a webpage, online store, or location that they can continue to pledge money to your campaign. To sum it up, you can use Spotlight not just to tell your story, but also to direct new customers to a link, be it your website or a place where they can buy your product or continue to support your campaign.

Indiegogo InDemand: As a reader mentioned, I have noticed an increasing trend of Kickstarter projects transitioning into the Indiegogo InDemand program. This has actually been happening for a while, and it makes sense. Indiegogo already has a thriving community of backers and being a part of the program gives creators more exposure than if they were simply on their own website. Also, it takes work to set up a whole new website to accept orders or pledges. Indiegogo makes it easy to continue to accept contributions.

When you enter the InDemand program, you don't have to set a fundraising goal or duration. You'll just update your title, tagline, video, pitch description, perks, etc. However, "You will not be able to edit your original funding goal, funding type, currency or any perks that have already been claimed." You'll receive distributions every 4 weeks and be charged the standard 5% + payment processing fees. You can still enter InDemand if you ran a Kickstarter project, however, the fee will be higher.

The big reasons to switch over to InDemand after running a Kickstarter campaign are for the convenience and to become a part of the Indiegogo marketplace. If you drive enough activity, you'll begin to see some promotion from Indiegogo. "We also regularly feature campaigns on our blog, newsletter, and social media channels."

Amazon: You can now sell your Kickstarted product on Amazon, as part of their new Kickstarter Collection section on Amazon Launchpad. It's pretty cool to see some of these projects that were "Made on Kickstarter." Scrolling down the list of these different products brings back a lot of memories. I've had several of the entrepreneurs behind these products on my podcast. It makes me smile to see how they've progressed.

Without a doubt, Amazon is the 2,000-pound gorilla in the ecommerce space. I think that this partnership that Amazon has made with Kickstarter creators is going to be good for both parties and lead to a lot of happy customers and business owners down the road. Not every entrepreneur has mastered driving traffic to their own website and being a part of a larger marketplace like Amazon is a great way to reap the benefits of continued exposure.

Shopify: If you want to drive traffic to your own website and accept orders or pre-orders, then Shopify is a no-brainer. A lot of entrepreneurs who have been on my podcast use Shopify to manage their online store. It's easy, relatively inexpensive, and there are a lot of great apps and themes that you have access to. For example, at the time of writing you could use the Pre-Order Manager app. Right now, Shopify costs $9/month for the most basic plan and $29/month for the basic business plan. They offer both free and premium themes that you can choose from when setting up your online store.

Wordpress: This is another popular option among readers and listeners. Most entrepreneurs will download the free open source version of WordPress and install it on a good hosting provider, like Bluehost (what I recommend) or HostGator. Then, they'll install the WooCommerce plugin which enables ecommerce functionality on your website. This will allow you to track sales data, accept payments, keep track of your inventory, manage taxes, and offer shipping. The great thing about WordPress is that you'll able to find lots of free and some very professional-looking premium themes online. WordPress has a big community, so there are also free and premium plugins that will expand on the functionality of your website.

Lesson #5: Don't Get a Big Head

On KickstarterForum, there have been 400+ replies since I asked the question "What is your day job? What is your passion project?"

After reading through 41 pages of replies, I've come to the conclusion that the majority of creators on Kickstarter have a full-time job and then their pet project or passion project on the side. Usually, they work on it after work or on the weekend. Considering that Kickstarter was founded in NYC and has their offices in Brooklyn, this is not surprising. Many New Yorkers have a full-time job and the passion project they are pursuing on the side, whether that's acting, comedy, writing, or a startup company.

Of course, a lot of creators love their full-time job and consider what they are doing on the side as more of a hobby. This post is more geared towards the creators who want to make that side project their primary gig. I've gathered a few bits of wisdom from personal experience that will increase the chance you can make that side project your primary focus and get paid for doing what you love.

First, you must seek to improve other people's lives. The only thing that matters is the degree to which you improve the quality of other people's lives. You can: solve problems they experience with a product or service, entertain them, or positively affect their life with a scaled service (radio, tv, blog, podcast). To full-time on our passion project, you can either:

1. Improve a large number of lives in a small way.

2. Improve a small number of lives in a big way.

3. Do both simultaneously.

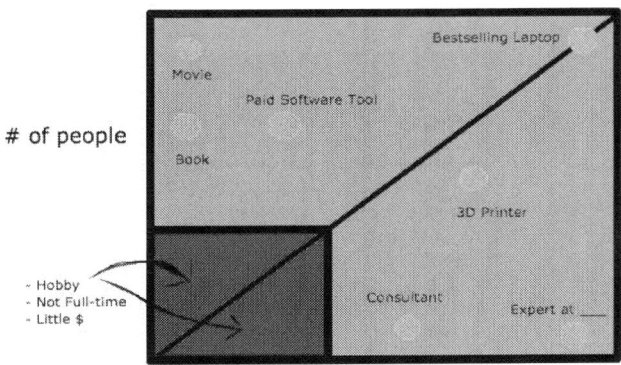

Amount you improve their life

Keep in mind that these are just examples. The main way I measure the amount that a product or service improves someone's life is how much they spent on it ($$$) and if they were happy with the purchase.

Example of #1: Create a book that entertains a reader for two weeks or the amount of time it takes them to finish it. It might cost $10 to buy the book. If a small number of people like the book, you won't have the funds to take time off work to go full-time on producing the next one. If a large number of people like it, you will. If you get $1.50 per book in royalties, you would need to sell ~20,000 per year to go full-time.

Example of #2: Create a new smart watch that is 10x better than existing models and solves pain points for users, particularly fitness lovers. If it retails at $250 and you are lucky enough to personally profit $100 per watch, you only need to sell 450 per year to make a living. Obviously, this is simplifying the manufacturing and human resource process, but you get the idea. The key here is that you are providing a lot of value over the lifetime of the watch to a small base of users (fitness lovers).

Example of #3: If you create an application like Facebook, write a blog, build up a YouTube channel, you will likely be providing a small amount of value for free to a large number of people. This value takes the form of helpful or entertaining content. You will also be providing a larger amount of value to a smaller number of people, which can take the form of paid advertisers or people who buy products that you've made, like an ebook, which comprise a smaller section of your audience.

The key here is that you need to provide enough value to your customers in order for you to go full-time on your creative work. You need to get out of the red box to go full-time on your side project. To get out of this red box, you can also be helpful to your audience in multiple ways. The easiest way to speed up going full-time on your project is to find new ways to serve your customer base or audience. Although most companies are founded on one product or service, rarely do companies survive on just one product or service. You can serve them in other ways.

How else can you improve their life, aside from the singular product that you are working on? A great example of an entrepreneur who finds new ways to please his customers is Dr. Dre, who not only is a rapper and music producer, but also created an awesome headphone company, Beats Electronics, which was bought by Apple for ~$3 billion. He has found multiple ways to serve people who like listening to music and over time, has increased the amount of people he serves and the amount that he improved their life.

Often times, improving a customer's life, even in a small way, will give them the feeling of trustworthiness that's needed to take a chance on your product or listen to your album. Never stop thinking of ways that you can provide value to your target market, whether that's through products or services. Ironically, this all comes from understanding your customers from an emotional perspective, not a logical perspective.

This goes for artists, creative types, and entrepreneurs. If you are writing a story that you don't intend to show to the world, then you need only write a storyline that you like. If you plan to share it with the world, then you need to think about whether or not they will like it and how it will move them. You need to get inside their head.

As an entrepreneur, one of the bigger mistakes that I've made has been to try to understand customers from an intellectual perspective, rather than an emotional perspective. Typically, when you're setting out with new projects the terms "business plans" "forecasting" and "customer archetype" come up frequently. The problem with these terms it that they pull you up to a bird's eye view of the battle field, rather than bringing you down to what's actually happening on the ground.

You must spend time with your customers and really try to feel what they are feeling. By being empathetic towards their problems, concerns, likes, desires, and dreams, you will increase the chances that you will create a product that they will love.

Here's one way to think about it. Intellectually, a customer might understand they should work out 3 times per week to lose fat and stay healthy, but whether they commit to that or not usually has to do with their emotional mindset. If you want to build a fitness product that will have a measurable impact on their behavior and thus get them results, you need to start with emotions rather than logic. Once you understand your customers or audience as well as you understand a family member, then you will have a much higher chance of creating a product that gets them results.

Finally, the fastest way to continue to grow your business after Kickstarter is to try things out and be okay with failing. Everyone hates failure, particularly public failure, but I've found that the fastest way to accumulate knowledge in an area is to try out a bunch of stuff and see what works, what fails, and why. If you launch a Kickstarter campaign, the only downside is that you'll learn more about marketing. If you raise a bunch of money, but fail to hit your goal, you'll have learned a heck of a lot about how people respond to your work. You'll see first-hand what they like and don't like.

Obviously, it's important to read everything you can get your hands on about your industry or niche, but at a certain point, the only other way to learn is through experimentation! The faster you are willing to learn, the quicker you're going to be able to get out of the part-time box and go full-time on your passion project. It's just like playing a hard-to-beat game on your smartphone. At first, you're going to die and fail miserably. After a while though, you'll be able to anticipate what's going to happen in the game and adjust yourself accordingly until you beat the first level. The faster you go through this learning cycle or the longer you play the game, the easier it becomes.

Remember, teenagers don't get good at video games because they naturally have better reflexes. They get better because they spend 10 hours at a sleepover playing the game non-stop with friends. You must strive for this level of effort and consistency. The enemy of all progress in life is inconstancy. When you're young, if you stop practicing a sport or musical instrument, you will fall behind. As you get older, if you want to lose weight, you need to stick to a diet and exercise regimen consistently over an extended period of time. You need to keep at it. In the same way that you might put aside money for your 401k, you must invest time in a goal. You must learn, create, and take action. If you do, it will compound over time, just like your financial investment, and soon you'll be working on your passion project full-time.

Chapter 8: Conclusion

There is a reason that the majority of new businesses fail in the first 1-5 years. There is a reason that most creative types aren't able to earn a living doing the type of work they love. You might hate me for saying this, but I'm going to, because it's true. With Kickstarter, business, or life, you have to be willing to put in the work if you expect to reap the rewards.

You've already taken a major step. You've read through some of the proven techniques and strategies in this guide. Now, you have to actually take action. You have to execute on your plan!

I have never spoken with a creator who regrets having put himself or herself out there, for all of the world to discover. Yeah, it might be hard at first, but almost every person I've spoken with actually wishes they did it sooner. Even if they failed the first time, they regret not having tried it earlier.

When I look back at my early blog posts, podcasts, or YouTube videos, I cringe. They are sooo bad. But, by trying things out, I quickly learned what worked, and what didn't. I figured out how to improve, and now, I've gained a whole new set of skills. I'm much more confident in my own abilities and I'm excited about a bright future that's filled with possibilities.

Thank you for spending a bit of time with me learning the ins and outs of Kickstarter, crowdfunding, and marketing. I consider it a privilege to be able to pass on some of my knowledge.

If you want to connect with me and gain access to more in-depth training material, don't forget to check out my FREE bonus Kickstarter training video (crowdcrux.com/kickstarterbonus)!

Happy Crowdfunding!

Salvador Briggman

"I learned many great lessons from my father, not the least of which was that you can fail at what you don't want, so you might as well take a chance on doing what you love." - Jim Carrey

About the Author

Salvador Briggman founded the popular blog, CrowdCrux, which has been cited by the New York Times, The Wallstreet Journal, CNN, and more. He helps entrepreneurs raise money on crowdfunding platforms like Kickstarter and Indiegogo. Last year, he helped nearly 400,000 individuals raise money from the crowd through his website, products, newsletter, and forum.

Printed in Great Britain
by Amazon